Judging Jesus

"Who do people say that I am?"

"You are God incarnate who redeems humanity."
"You are a blasphemer and the offspring of an adulterous woman."
"You are, indeed, a Messenger of God."
"You are a manifestation of the Divine."
"You are an enlightened being, a teacher of great truths."
"Your story is a portrayal of how to live a truly human life."
"You are a great and good man, but you do not exceed other great and good men in human virtues."

Judging Jesus

World Religions' Answers to "Who Do People Say That I Am?"

Wayne G. Johnson

Hamilton Books

An Imprint of
Rowman & Littlefield
Lanham • Boulder • New York • Toronto • Plymouth, UK

Copyright © 2016 by Hamilton Books
4501 Forbes Boulevard, Suite 200, Lanham, Maryland 20706
Hamilton Books Acquisitions Department (301) 459-3366

Unit A, Whitacre Mews, 26-34 Stannary Street,
London SE11 4AB, United Kingdom

All rights reserved
Printed in the United States of America
British Library Cataloguing in Publication Information Available

Library of Congress Control Number: 2016948979
ISBN: 978-0-7618-6836-1 (pbk : alk. paper)—ISBN: 978-0-7618-6837-8 (electronic)

∞™ The paper used in this publication meets the minimum requirements of American National Standard for Information Sciences Permanence of Paper for Printed Library Materials, ANSI/NISO Z39.48-1992.

To my children:
Susan, Scott, Jeffrey, and Jonathan,
major characters in my life story;
and to Marge,
loving companion in later life chapters

Contents

Foreword		ix
1	The Stories by Which We Live	1
2	Jesus in Christianity	11
3	Jesus in Judaism	37
4	Jesus in Islam	55
5	Jesus in Hinduism	69
6	Jesus in Buddhism	81
7	Jesus Only? Religions and the Fate of Others	91
Bibliography		115
Index		119

Foreword

Human history is awash in a sea of religions. These religions are carried through history by way of stories that ground and direct the lives of the faithful. The image of a sea of religions suggests that there is something about life experience that inclines human beings toward religious beliefs and practices. Some of the stories may be true in some significant sense of *true*; but the important factor is that they be *believed*.

Aside from undertaking the persistent struggle to stay alive, we *Homo sapiens* are blessed—or cursed—with levels of intelligence and consciousness that open us up to a variety of concerns and stresses. For one, there is the haunting riddle of death. All animals die; but perhaps only human beings become aware of that fact—that *they, themselves,* must some day die. This knowledge brings a certain passion to their lives as they seek some answer to that riddle. All religions provide just such answers in great variety. For thousands of years there have also been non-religious voices that spoke to that concern.

But the problem of death is not the only riddle. We also seek meaning for this human venture—some point to our life. Linked to that quest is the need for community—for acceptance, for affirmation, for self-respect, for love. The list could be extended, but these basic needs are always addressed in the great religions.

These various human needs suggest a marketplace model of religion. Religious systems compete, directly or indirectly, for believing customers. This view of religion was reflected in a comment made by a man attending a presentation exploring the Protestant faith. To speak of Protestantism is to speak about the influence of St. Paul. As Paul's views were explored, the man suggested, somewhat facetiously, "Paul was a good salesman." An appropriate response in the same marketplace image could have been, "Yes—

and some thought that he had a good product." Others, of course, declined Paul's religious merchandise.

Competition among religions is one of the themes of this book. When the Christian story about Jesus encounters religions that are already in place, those who hold beliefs in a different story find themselves challenged. They may become interested in this new story that has been presented to them. Responses are then required. This work explores responses that range from complete rejection of the Christian story to an adoption of part of the story by folding Jesus into a faith story already held. The invitation to a new faith—the work of missionaries—represents a challenge to beliefs already held. It is of no surprise, therefore, that the responses are sometimes extremely hostile. Wars of the mind and spirit develop. At other times, wars of physical violence at various levels ensue.

Tracing this competition reveals the supremacist tendency in every world religion. Sincere believers of every faith—including secular faiths—generally believe that they hold a privileged position, that they are closer than others to important truths. This seems a reasonable belief since it would seem odd, if not self-contradictory, for someone to be committed to a faith that he or she believed was inferior to another faith. This supremacist tendency is reflected in a variety of self-designations: the "elect," the "enlightened," the "chosen," the "straight path." Serious religious faith is not a trivial matter for those believing.

Tracing this religious competition also reveals a tribalism that seems deeply embedded in human nature. We find an important part of our identity linked to a tribal structure of which we are a part. Tribal loyalties of various kinds are possible—nationalistic, ethnic, racial, political, and religious. Even sporting events reveal tribalism; few Green Bay Packer fans cheer for the Chicago Bears. Charles Darwin suggested that tribalism has an evolutionary advantage in that a tribe made up of members deeply committed to and willing to die for their tribe will probably be victorious in clashes with enemy tribes.

Loyalty is a highly praised virtue. This tribalism is also reflected in national narratives during times of stress when a religious dimension is injected. Politicians often end their stump speeches with something like, "And may God bless America!" One significant facet of this book is the examination of how religious tribalism is negotiated. The patterns range from deep hostility to warm tolerance, if not outright conversion.

Some cautionary notes must be expressed. (1) This work is intended to be purely descriptive and objective. I have tried to avoid any suggestion that one religious story is superior to any other. I leave it to each religion to make its supremacist claim in its own way. This book is an attempt to inform, not to persuade. (2) This work is not to be construed as a history of religion or comparative religion text. I attempt brief summaries of various religions in order to show significant distinctions between the Christian story and a competing faith. These brief summaries cannot claim to represent the breadth and depth of these often complex faiths. A list of suggested readings in endnotes may be of help to those who find their interest heightened. (3) In order to moderate the length of this book, I needed to be quite selective in choosing the voices from the various faiths that have responded to the Christian story. I sought to find voices that represented the spectrum available in each responding faith. It became clear that no one voice or group could speak for the entire faith community. (4) The chapter on Jesus in Christianity was a special challenge. That topic could easily involve a work of encyclopedic length. Therefore, I chose to first trace the variety of voices—often conflicting—that finally formed the early creeds of Christianity. This is followed by a review of some highly influential figures in traditional Christianity. Then I trace lines of thought from those who strayed from the classic creedal forms of Christianity and envisioned a different path onto which their Jesus led them.

The question still remains: "Who do people say that I am?" For many in the twenty-first century, this is still a life-challenging and serious question. For a variety of reasons the question is, at best, of only historical interest or intellectual curiosity to others. Whether or not the question is a vital one for you, the reader, it is my hope you will gain some sense of the weight of that question as it impinged on the lives of many. Our blue planet is the home for a sea of faith stories. Our own lives can be enriched through a better understanding of the voyages of those who share our little spot in the universe.

Chapter One

The Stories by Which We Live

"In the beginning . . ." (Genesis 1:1; John 1:1)

Few individuals have had as much impact on human history as Jesus of Nazareth. His influence raises the question of the nature of a Great Man or Woman. Is history shaped largely by the impact of unique individuals? Or are these individuals the product of a society in an historical setting that made their lives and greatness possible? How does one best account for figures like Alexander the Great, Plato, Cleopatra, the Buddha, Elizabeth the First, Napoleon, and Abraham Lincoln? These issues were raised in the late nineteenth century by Thomas Carlyle, who proffered a "Great Man" theory of history. In response, Herbert Spencer argued that the historical setting was the dominant factor.[1]

JESUS AS A GREAT MAN

Jesus of Nazareth would be a fruitful focus for just such a debate. The four Gospels in the New Testament place Jesus solidly within the culture of Palestinian Judaism under Roman rule. A spate of books pursuing "the quest for the historical Jesus" tends, also, to confirm that Jesus was indeed a Jew.[2] Thus, much can be said for the role of the historical and social setting in the making of Jesus as a Great Man. Nevertheless, various sources claim that there was something unique about this man from Nazareth that cannot be explained solely on the basis of the historical setting. Many of his followers have grounded this uniqueness in his divine status. While this book will not take part in the Great Man debate, it will trace how the major world religions have viewed this Jesus. Voices from these religions evaluate this *Great Man*.

However *Great* Jesus came to be, his initial impact was quite limited. Although he evidently caught the attention of throngs at times, standard sources suggest that a group of twelve men were the first close followers. Furthermore, these men appear to have beaten a retreat at his arrest and crucifixion. The cruelty of Roman justice was palpable. Now, almost 2100 years later, the movement numbers some 2.2 billion followers who proclaim him in some way as *Teacher, Master, Savior, Messiah (Christ).* Many historians would consider this man to be the most important figure of history in terms of his influence. His light—or shadow—falls on almost all aspects of civilization: religious beliefs, philosophy, literature, architecture, music, the visual arts, and science as well. More books have been written about Jesus than any other man or woman. If it were possible to extract all these influences from the history of the world, our civilization would present a graphically different picture.

While his influence has been monumental, the man and the movement he inspired are not without detractors and opponents. While it can be argued that much good has come from the followers of Jesus, history also records conflicts and cruelty related to, if not always directly caused by, his followers. He has been loved. He has also, though rarely, been reviled. His followers have certainly drawn criticism.

One way of tracing the influence of Jesus upon human history would be to explore how world religions view the man and his message. In a certain sense, the question that Jesus directed to his disciples still calls for an answer: "Who do people say that I am?" (Mark 8:18, parallels in Matt. 16:13, and Luke 9:18) This work will trace answers given by voices from the major world religions.

WORLD SCRIPTURES: *BY* FAITH AND *FOR* FAITH

An interpretive pattern will emerge throughout the coming chapters. The sacred scriptures of various world religions can all be seen as documents written *by* faith *for* faith. They are invitations to believe and to participate, not arguments designed to establish sound conclusions. A line from the Gospel of John expresses this directly: "But these are written so that you may come to believe [not *know*] that Jesus is the Messiah, the Son of God, and that through believing you may have life in his name." (John 20:31) The Torah (Judaism) and the Quran (Islam) present much the same type of message to their hearers or readers. Buddhist and Hindu scriptures would not be exceptions to this pattern.

HUMAN BEINGS AS STORYTELLERS

A second interpretive pattern will also emerge in the chapters that follow. As far as we know, human beings appear to be the only species that tells stories. We are, by nature, storytelling animals—perhaps from the very early stages of our evolution. Cave drawings by our early ancestors suggest storytelling through art. In our own societies stories abound from the relaxed chatter over lunch, the movies viewed, the novels read, the plays and operas attended, the gossip shared. Social and political movements gain much of their impact through stories told. Each of us comes to a sense of personal identity by way of the stories we hear from those who nurtured us. To lose such stories, for example, through complete loss of memory, would be to lose all sense of who we are.[3]

The significance of stories in the lives of human beings lies not so much in the *truth* of such stories, but in their effectiveness. Since this is often the case, the historical or actual truth of the story may be difficult to establish. Politicians and orators know that instinctively, if not consciously. Fiction illustrates this point. Harriet Beecher Stowe's *Uncle Tom's Cabin* had an enormous impact in the U.S. and internationally on the slavery issue. The works of Charles Dickens helped remedy the plight of the poor in England. The Rabbinical tradition in Judaism was rich in storytelling, a teaching tool reflected in the New Testament accounts of the life of Jesus.

This storytelling is strikingly present in the myths of the ancient Greeks. Scholars refer to a "mythopoeic mind" (mythmaking mind), which preceded a more theoretical approach to the world of thought. This mythopoeic stage of human thought saw the events of the world as actions carried out by gods, goddesses, and other spirits. These myths functioned as both their science and their religion. The *causes* of events in the world were linked to the will of these various beings, not to some law-abiding structure within the stuff of nature itself.[4]

Scholars also note that myths are an important part of world religions. Stories about the Buddha's birth and his temptations abound. The Hindu scriptures are full of stories about gods and goddesses. Jewish and Christian scriptures present two stories, or myths, that explain the origin of the earth with its various forms of life. The flood story of Noah tells of an angry God wreaking vengeance upon a wicked humanity. The book of Exodus recounts the story of God bringing his people out of Egypt into a promised land. In the Mormon faith, there is the story of the discovery of the golden tablets by Joseph Smith. Christian gospels proclaim the story of the virgin birth.

MYTHS: LIVE AND DEAD

While the term "myth" may be unsettling to some believers, scholars usually use the term without any judgment regarding the *truth* of such stories. "Myths" are stories about the activities of supernatural beings. Theologian Paul Tillich provides an analysis of various possible attitudes regarding myths.[5] Instead of viewing myths in terms of being true or false, Tillich suggests that they be seen as either *live* or *dead*. A live myth is a story that carries some significant meaning for an individual, while a dead myth may be an historical curiosity but carries no personal meaning. The status of dead or live is, then, in the mind of the individual person, not based on some kind of objective judgment. For most people of European descent, the Hindu myths in the Bhagavad-Gita would be dead myths, while the Genesis creation stories may be live for some.

Tillich continues his analysis by positing that live myths can fall into three possible categories: *natural literalism, reactive literalism,* or *broken*. A myth has the status of natural literalism for an individual if that individual understands the myth to be true in a literal sense without being aware that such stories may be symbolic. For that person, the myth portrays an event that actually took place in history. The creation stories in Genesis are, for some, taken as live myths in this literal way. However, once a reader of these stories has been exposed to the possibility of symbolic meanings for myths, that individual can no longer exist in the natural literalism mode.

Now the reader must make a choice. One choice would be that of reactive literalism wherein a literal view of the myth would be deliberately retained and the possibility of symbolic meaning would be rejected. Fundamentalists of various traditions tend to adopt reactive literalism, often with a great deal of passion.

Another choice would be to agree with the suggestion and opt for a symbolic rather than a literal meaning. If that second option is taken, then the individual views the myth as a broken myth. Again, by "broken," Tillich means only that the literalness of the story has been rejected, but the myth is still live in the sense that it carries significant meaning. Many people in various religions find the broken myth view to be compatible with their religious beliefs. Some Christians and Jews, for instance, would not view the Genesis creation stories as literal descriptions of historical events, but as expressions of the faith conviction that ultimate origins are rooted in God.

THE POWER OF STORIES

Sociologist Robert Bellah wrote, "Families, nations, religions (but also corporations, universities, departments of sociology) know who they are by the stories they tell."[6] National stories become central and powerful in times of war. Stories, then, move persons to commitments that involve the risk of life and to efforts designed to secure safety for the nation. "The Star Spangled Banner," as poem and national anthem, tells a story that can move even the most hardened Americans to tears. National stories are often told to ensure that those who have died for the nation's cause will not have died in vain. Finally, the stories told by nations almost always involve religious dimensions that bind the citizen to the highest form of loyalty. Popular songs in various nations during great wars often reflect just such religious affirmations: "God Bless America" and "America the Beautiful" are prime examples.

The great religions proclaim their message by stories. Believers are those who come to share and be part of that particular story. For example, the Torah of Judaism sets the story's tone in the opening lines: "In the beginning when God created the heavens and the earth, the earth was a formless void and darkness covered the face of the deep, while a wind from God swept over the face of the waters." (Gen. 1:1–2)

The Gospel of John echoes this story line in a different key: "In the beginning was the Word, and the Word was with God, and the Word was God." (John 1:1) Throughout the synoptic gospels (Matthew, Mark, and Luke) Jesus uses stories in the form of parables as a major way of communicating his message. This theme of faith as story is effectively developed in a work by three scholars in *Mark as Story: An Introduction to the Narrative of a Gospel*. The work investigates the oral traditions (stories) reflected in the Gospel of Mark and demonstrates the power of that Gospel when read and recited as "story."[7]

RELIGIONS AS MEMES

Another way of examining the stories involved in various religious traditions is to view these stories as *memeplexes*, a complex of *memes*. "Meme" is a term invented by Richard Dawkins in *The Selfish Gene* and is defined as "an idea, behavior, or style that spreads from person to person within a culture."[8] Memes act as units which carry beliefs, ideas, and practices from one person to another and also from culture to culture. As they spread, the memes of one culture can be challenged by memes of another culture or by memes generated within its own culture.[9] Even so, religious stories, as memes, challenge other religious stories.

Proponents of the concept of memes suggest that memes are caught up in evolutionary processes just as genes are. Memes survive—or fail to survive—within cultures. And memes often survive or die out in the face of environmental pressures—such as other memes—by way of variation and mutation. The theory that the earth is at the center of our solar system is a meme that has lost its status. The heliocentric view of our solar system is a meme that has caused the demise of the geocentric meme. Science, itself, is a complex meme.

Religions as memes survive or fail to survive in the face of other religions or other beliefs. They survive either by successfully rejecting the challenging belief or by *evolving* through interpretive variation that helps the meme (story) survive in the face of a possible threat. For example, in the last two centuries, various religions have had to come to terms with new scientific claims. For many, the Adam and Eve story can no longer function as a literal account of the first human beings. Alternative explanations of those Genesis stories have been offered. This process of interpretive variation breeds orthodoxy as well as heresy. Sects can be seen as mutations from a parent meme. A religion may also manage to survive not by evolving but by petrifaction if the petrified result manages to be sustainable in the face of cultural changes and challenges.

The function of religious memes and their challenges are brilliantly portrayed in the play and film *Fiddler on the Roof*. The story involves a small Jewish community in Russia in the late nineteenth century trying to survive in the face of mounting anti-Semitism and other challenges. Tevye, the main character, maintains that their traditions help Jews not only to know who they are as individuals and as a people but also to know what God expects of them.[10] Tradition gives them identity and a way of life. Tevye has five daughters, three of whom come to illustrate the challenge to the meme of their Jewish tradition. One daughter marries out of love instead of marrying the man chosen by her father. Another daughter leaves the community to join her revolutionary lover who is committed to a cause other than their tradition. And the younger daughter leaves the faith altogether by converting and marrying a man of Eastern Orthodox Christian faith. This event prompts Tevye to the painful choice of rejecting his daughter altogether since she has left the faith. Yet the little community moves on, forced out of its town by anti-Semitic pressures. For the faithful, the meme survives. They will await the Messiah in some other land.

The power and significance of a religious meme are concisely expressed by historian Paul Johnson: "The Jews believed they were a special people with such unanimity and passion, and over so long a span, that they became one. They did indeed have a role because they wrote it for themselves. There, perhaps, lies the key to their story."[11]

A philosophical observation at this point is appropriate. The above material that refers to religions as *stories* or *myths* or *memes* does not entail the conclusion that such stories, myths, or memes are false beliefs. Such a conclusion would require more true premises. One could, however, venture the claim that not *all* of the world religions can be true. It is also possible that all are false. Or perhaps one of them could be true. These issues are beyond the purview of this book.

RELIGION AS A QUEST FOR "SALVATION"

Another element in world religions to be explored relates to what may well be the essential aim of all religious traditions. This central aim is to find the most fulfilling way to respond to the human experience. All religious faiths agree that human experience typically involves trials, loss, and suffering. In the story of Siddhartha Gautama—who became the Buddha—"four passing sights" made him acutely aware of the problematic nature of human life. The first three sights were of old age, sickness, and death. The fourth sight was that of a monk seeking peace in this troubled world. The human dilemma is also expressed on ancient Roman gravestones reflecting Epicurean philosophy: "Non fui, fui, non sum, non curo." (I was not, I was, I am not, I do not care.)

While expressed in differing ways, religions tend to agree that somehow things are not as they could be; the world is broken or out of joint or fallen. Many cultures have stories that account for this state of affairs. The common one in the Biblical tradition is the story of the fall of Adam and Eve in the Garden of Eden. This story suggests that there was, once, a better time and that the present world situation in which we live is not as it could be or might be.

World religions agree that the human situation is challenging. They also agree that there is an adequate response to that situation, and each religion claims to supply it through its story. The questions raised by the human condition—such as death, suffering, guilt, meaninglessness—are answered by way of religious affirmations.

In responding to the human condition, religions tend to differ in two ways: They differ in their *diagnosis* of the fundamental human problem; and they differ in their *prescription* of the answer to that problem. The religious *answer* must correlate with the diagnosis of the *problem*. If a religious message is to be meaningful to an individual, that message must relate to the problem experienced by that individual. Clergy of all faiths realize this connection whenever they seek to assist those who are suffering, such as those whose child died or those who find life empty of meaning.

World religions hold views about the fundamental problem of the human condition that differ from the view held by Christianity. The question to be raised, then, is whether or not the Christian story provides a viable answer to the problems as diagnosed by other religions. Is the message about Jesus an adequate response to the human condition as viewed by Jews, Muslims, Hindus, or Buddhists?

In the sea of world religions, Jesus's question remains: "Who do people say that I am?" Answers will come from these traditions in a form that relates, in some way, to their own story. All religions, other than Christianity, would presumably *not* reply, "You are the Christ, the Savior and Redeemer of humankind." That answer would place them as participants in the traditional Christian story. They would no longer be Jew, Muslim, Hindu, or Buddhist. Keeping to a non-Christian tradition or story requires a response that in some way rejects the traditional Christian story.

THE HISTORICAL JESUS AND THE CHRIST OF FAITH

In tracing the views of Jesus held by various world religions, it becomes necessary to make a distinction between two narratives about him. One is the traditional narrative of the *Christ of Faith* that enfolds Jesus into classic Christian doctrine as the Son of God, born of the Virgin Mary, part of the Trinity, redeemer of those who trust in him, and the righteous judge at the end of days. The other view is that of the man of Nazareth, teacher of high morality, who is sometimes referred to as the *historical Jesus*.

This distinction between these two narratives about Jesus involves another distinction—the religion *about* Jesus, and the religion *of* Jesus. The religion *about* Jesus is expressed in the classic creeds of Christianity—the Christ of Faith—professed by Christians for most of the first seventeen centuries of the faith. The religion *of* Jesus is linked to the "quest for the historical Jesus" that emerged in the Enlightenment movement of the eighteenth century. This quest was the attempt to retrieve, as clearly as possible, the religious beliefs expressed *by* Jesus during his ministry. Thomas Jefferson, for instance, largely rejected the creeds attached to the Christ of Faith but honored the historical Jesus as "the first of human Sages."[12]

The Christian narrative that first encountered other religions of the world was the story of the Christ of Faith. These religions were confronted by a religion *about* Jesus, not the religion *of* Jesus himself. Given that the first Christian message brought to other world religions was that of the Christ of Faith, voices from these religions expressed a variety of responses: (1) They developed counternarratives about Jesus himself that sought to expose him as corrupt or fraudulent. (2) They judged Christian doctrine *about* Jesus to be in conflict with their own religious affirmations and, therefore, rejected the entire package of Christianity. (3) They found the Christian doctrine *about* Jesus to be irrational and, therefore, rejected the entire Christian story. (4) They rejected Christian doctrine *about* Jesus and yet found in him a teacher worthy of respect insofar as his moral insights could be incorporated into their own moral affirmations.

In gospel accounts, Jesus asks of his disciples, "Who do people say that I am?" (Mark 8:18) The following chapters expand on these responses from voices within the five great world religions:

"You are God incarnate who redeems humanity."
"You are a blasphemer and the offspring of an adulterous woman."
"You are, indeed, a Messenger of God"
"You are a manifestation of the Divine."
"You are an enlightened being, a teacher of great truths."
"Your story is a portrayal of how to live a truly human life."
"You are a great and good man, but you do not exceed other great and good men in human virtues."

NOTES

1. For the early discussion, see Thomas Carlyle, *On Heroes, Hero Worship and the Heroic in History* (New York: Fredrick A. Stokes & Brother, 1888); and Herbert Spencer, *The Study of Sociology* (New York: Appleton, 1996).

2. For an early work on this topic, see Albert Schweitzer, *The Quest of the Historical Jesus: A Critical Study of the Progress from Reimarus to Wrede* (New York: Macmillan, 1906). For a current review of a variety of positions, see Mark Powell, *Jesus as a Figure of History* (Louisville, Kentucky: Westminster John Knox Press, 1988).

3. For an account of the significance of stories, see Yuval Harari, *Sapiens: A Brief History of Mankind* (New York: Harper Collins, 2015), 24–32. For the significance of story (narrative) in religion, see Robert Bellah, *Religion in Human Evolution* (Cambridge: Harvard University Press, 2011), 44 f.

4. See H. A. Frankfort, Before *Philosophy: The Intellectual Adventure of Ancient* Man (Chicago: University of Chicago Press, 1977).

5. Paul Tillich, *The Dynamics of Faith* (New York: Harper and Row, 1957).

6. Bellah, 35.

7. David Rhoads, Joanna Dewey, and Donald Michie, *Mark as Story: An Introduction to the Narrative of the Gospel* (Minneapolis, MN: Augsburg Fortress Press, 2012).

8. *Merriam-Webster Collegiate Dictionary* (Springfield, MA: Merriam-Webster, Incorporated, eleventh edition, 2014).

9. For a developed account of the significance of memes, see Susan Blackmore, *The Meme Machine* (Oxford: Oxford University Press, 1999).

10. The play and film are based on Sholom Aleichem, *Tevye's Daughters: Collected Stories of Sholom Aleichem* (New York: Crown Publishers, Frances Butwin, translator, 1949).

11. Paul Johnson, *A History of the Jews* (New York: Harper Perennial, 1988), 587.

12. Stephen Prothero, *American Jesus: How the Son of God Became a National Icon* (New York: Farrar, Straus and Giroux, 2003), 23. For an extensive exploration of the distinction between the religion *of* Jesus and the religion *about* Jesus, see Paula Fredriksen, *From Jesus to Christ: the Origins of the new Testament Images of Christ* (New Haven: Yale University Press, 1998), and L. Michael White, *From Jesus to Christianity* (New York: HarperCollins, 2004).

Chapter Two

Jesus in Christianity

Like all great world religions, the Christian story did not come forth fully born. While rooted in the events surrounding the life and death of Jesus of Nazareth, the Christian story was developed in a variety of ways by those who claimed him as Rabbi, Master, Lord, Messiah (Christ), and Savior. The name "Jesus" is derived from the Greek version of the Hebrew "Yeshua." "Christ" (from the Greek) is a *title* rather than a name and represents a Greek translation of the Hebrew "Messiah." Early followers of Jesus believed he was the Messiah (Christ) of the Jewish hope. In common usage, the title "Christ" now often functions as another *name* for Jesus rather than a title. This chapter explores some of the many voices that helped create the Christian story about Jesus and his titles. It is a story about how the man Jesus became proclaimed as the Christ.[1]

A complicating factor is the problem of definition. Just what constitutes being a "Christian"? A variety of creeds were promulgated in the early centuries in an attempt to clarify this question in the light of the controversies of the day. Later in history, a cluster of confessions of faith and proclamations attempted to provide guidance for members of various churches and sects as they pursued their own convictions.

DEFINING "CHRISTIAN"

Rather than define "Christian" in terms of clear doctrine or confessions, a dictionary definition suggests an approach: "Christian n. 1a: One who professes belief in the teachings of Jesus Christ."[2] Reformulating that suggestion, this chapter will consider a Christian as "a person who holds Jesus as the central factor of his or her religious faith and life." Such a definition provides some focus but also allows for the vagueness necessary to enlarge the scope. The definition proposes a "big tent" or broad view of Christianity, which can include the most orthodox creedal positions as well as Enlightenment views such as those of Thomas Jefferson.[3]

This definition may appear too broad since it would include early figures—later ruled as heretics—into the tent. Nevertheless, including these individuals will help provide a clearer picture of how Christian leaders sought to relate their message to beliefs alive in that Hellenistic world. Religious groups—like many other groups—often define themselves in opposition to other groups. Even so, Christian orthodoxy grew out of conflict with opposing views that were eventually deemed as heretical.

This big tent definition of "Christian" could ultimately include an excessive number of persons and groups who have self-identified as followers of Jesus. Hence, this chapter must be selective. The variety of views that appeared in the early centuries of the Christian movement will be traced first. This will take the story through the formulation of the basic creeds and theological themes that established what could be called Christian orthodoxy. As centuries passed, these creeds were challenged in a variety of ways resulting in a proliferation of churches, sects, and cults. At that point, only a few representative persons and groups that came onto the scene will be noted. No doubt some significant voices will be omitted.

While the life and teachings of Jesus are a significant story in its own right, that subject matter will not be traced in this chapter. Instead, this chapter focuses on how Jesus himself is viewed by a variety of persons and groups who identified themselves as followers.[4] In pursuing this focus, this chapter describes how the Christian story *about* Jesus and his significance gradually developed outside of its original Palestinian setting and how the developed Christian story *about* Jesus moved beyond what Jesus himself taught.

RELIGION IN THE ANCIENT WORLD

Before tracing the development of the Christian story of and about Jesus, a survey of the religious scene in that ancient world will be helpful. The early followers of Jesus made use of ideas and beliefs they found meaningful and that would also be meaningful to anticipated converts. This approach was particularly important as the Jesus Movement shifted its focus from Jerusalem to the Hellenistic world of the Roman Empire.[5] The Christian message needed to speak to basic religious needs of those invited into the new faith. That ancient world was afloat in a great sea of religions, cults, and philosophical speculations, all of which reflected attempts to deal with such human needs.

The peoples of that ancient world faced the perennial challenges of human life. The goddess of Fate (Greek *Tyche*, Latin *Fortuna*) was widely worshipped and feared. Often portrayed as blind and totally arbitrary, Fate represented the precarious nature of human experience. The need for security and the physical necessities of life were probably primary, as in all ages, but the quests for respect, justice, joy, and love are always basic to the human venture.

There is also the inevitable problem of death. While all creatures eventually die, it may well be that human beings are the only creatures that come to *realize* that they, themselves, will die. The full realization of that fact usually comes to children near the end of their first decade, which is also the traditional age for children to be formally inducted into religious groups. Yet it also seems possible for individuals to construct a psychological *denial* of the fact that they, too, will someday die.[6] Linked to the problem of death is also the question of the meaning of life. What is the point of it all—if any? The ancient world into which the Christian message moved was brimming with a wide variety of religions and philosophies that sought to bring adequate responses to all such human questions and needs.

To accomplish a meaningful connection with peoples in the wider Greco-Roman world, early Christians incorporated into their message traditions or systems of thought that were known in their time and place. These would include the Jewish traditions and the Hebrew Scriptures (Old Testament) available to them in a Greek translation, the Septuagint. Also included would be forms of thought from a cluster of ancient religious myths as well as works more philosophical in nature from Greek and Roman writers.

JUDAISM IN THE TIME OF JESUS

Within Judaism at that time were a variety of sects holding contrasting beliefs. It therefore is appropriate to speak in terms of many *Judaisms* instead of a singular Judaism. Core themes from within that spectrum of beliefs were incorporated into the Christian message. These would include an ethical monotheism involving only one God as creator and ultimately ruler of the world and of history. This God establishes moral guidelines, with promise of reward or punishment, for individuals and communities. For those who failed the moral guidelines, there were means established to attain cleansing and forgiveness through rituals and sacrifices, including blood sacrifices.

Two significant parties within Judaism at that time were the Sadducees and the Pharisees. In contrast to the Sadducees, the Pharisees held that the dead would someday be resurrected to face a judgment that determines their eternal destiny, which could include either a great fulfillment or punishment. The Sadducees, a more conservative party, rejected the idea of the resurrection of the dead and a meaningful life in the World to Come. They rejected these doctrines because they were not expressed in the Torah, the basic scriptures for the Jews. Throughout Judaism there was a Messianic hope expressed in a variety of often contradictory ways. One hope was for a Messiah who would defeat the enemies of God's people and restore the Kingdom of the Jews. Another hope was for a Messiah who would bring about the fulfillment of all history in a new peaceful world.

GREEK AND ROMAN RELIGION

Beliefs from the Greek and Roman cultures were also available for adaptation or rejection by the new faith. There were gods many and saviors many. The gods of Greece and Rome functioned as a way of thinking about the cosmic order of things. Gods, for instance, controlled the seas, others controlled the fertility of the earth, and others were related to the birth of children. If there were one divine reality, it appeared as though that Being had sublet various governing responsibilities to a variety of lesser gods. In addition to these cosmic powers, gods also functioned as patron deities of a city or a state. Since all such deities were looked upon as protectors of cities or states, the citizens were expected to perform rites to honor such gods. Piety was a civic virtue and requirement. Parallels in our present world scene are not difficult to identify since nations and peoples often declare that God is on their side.

The gods of Greece and Rome were portrayed in anthropomorphic (human-like) terms, which included sexual exploits and the procreation of children among the gods and between gods and human beings. The concept of "sons of god" would have been familiar. In his own day, for instance, Caesar Augustus was not declared a "god," but he was called a "son of god" in reference to Julius Caesar who had been raised to the divine level after his death.

The personal needs of individual citizens, however, were seldom addressed in the rites related to the gods of city or empire. The state and city gods of Roman paganism, such as Jupiter and Juno, had little to offer in the way of intense personal experience. Given their evident propensity for jealousy, envy, wrath, and lust, these gods were more feared than regarded as moral role models. They had long been criticized by Greek philosophers. Nor did the rituals and rites related to these gods provide anything like a community of support and caring. There appeared to be a great religious hunger that needed to be fed.

Various cults and movements sought to appease this hunger. Often originating in Egypt, cults and religions migrated into Greece and Rome and were generally modified in this new setting. The scene resembled something like a free enterprise marketplace of religions, all appealing to various constituents and "customers."[7] While there were official gods and goddesses of the Empire and cities, there was no absolute power that enforced one faith and restrained others. That came later when Roman emperors converted to Christianity. But during the years of early Christianity, there were a multitude of religious options and a general sense of tolerance by the Empire as long as a religious group did not bring about social unrest. This setting was fertile ground for new religious cults and sects that appealed to deep human needs.

The cult that developed around Cybele, known as the Great Mother to the Romans, apparently fed a need for intense personal experience, a need often expressed in religious movements. Myths linked to Cybele, a goddess of fertility for plants and animals, involved episodes of death and rebirth related to the sexual indiscretions of her lover, Attis. Worship rituals included ecstatic frenzies that led to the self-castration of priests of the cult.[8] Another rite involved a ritual of cleansing wherein initiates were drenched in the blood of a sacrificed bull giving them a new life.

Other myths from Greece and Rome served to explain the movement of the seasons from new life in the spring, followed by harvest and the "death" of winter and "rebirth" *again* in the spring. Such myths were also expanded to include the prospect of death and rebirth for those initiated into various cults. The story of Demeter, the goddess of grain and harvest, and her daughter Persephone traced the abduction of Persephone by Hades into his deathly kingdom. With the help of Zeus, a high god, she is released from the underworld kingdom but was tricked so that she had to return to the realm of Hades for a period each year. Beginning as an etiological myth (myth of origins) to explain the origins of the seasons of the year, the cult of Demeter expanded to become the symbol of personal immortality for those initiated into the cult.

The religion related to the myths of Isis and Osiris came close to reflecting a type of monotheism. The original myth reflected the agrarian cycle of the Nile River in Egypt but expanded to include the promise of immortality and a blessed afterlife for those initiated into the cult. The followers of Isis, known as the Queen of Heaven, tended to form congregations that set themselves apart from the larger society and gave mutual support to the members. While they did not deny the existence of other gods, they worshipped Isis as the supreme god figure.

Adaptations from this wide variety of traditions and systems of thought by early Christians also provided seeds for conflict within the developing Christian community. This conflict resulted in various views, some of which attained orthodox belief while others were ultimately deemed heretical by church leaders.

EARLY CHRISTIAN STRUGGLES

The early years of the Jesus Movement were marked by hardships and internal tensions. Some of the early Jewish Christians were persecuted by Jews who looked upon the new faith as a dangerous heresy. The New Testament Book of Acts, Chapter 7, recounts the stoning to death of Stephen, the first Christian martyr, at the hands of the Sanhedrin—a body of Jewish judges that made many decisions for the Jewish community during Roman rule. At that time, Jewish law allowed for blasphemers to be stoned to death. Another account of persecution comes from the Jewish historian, Josephus, who recorded in his *Antiquities* that James, the brother of Jesus, was arrested and executed by the high priest Ananus around 62 CE.[9]

After the destruction of Jerusalem by the Romans in 70 CE in response to Jewish revolutionaries, Jews were forced out of the city. The fate of the Jewish Christians in Jerusalem at that time is unclear. A passage from Josephus may have recorded their fate at the hands of Roman troops as they stormed the Temple. But a later gentile (non-Jew) church tradition held that these Jewish Christians fled *before* the Roman siege.[10] This event largely ended the influence of that young Jewish-Christian Jerusalem movement. The growing frontier of the new faith now moved into the Greco-Roman world of the Roman Empire. It was in that ancient Hellenistic world where both early Christians and the Jews sought to clarify the meaning of this Jesus of Nazareth. For those early Christians, a central set of experiences and beliefs—stories of the life and teachings of Jesus, his crucifixion, and the resurrection experience—appear to have been shared. The impact of the man already had made a deep mark, but more developed formulations of the message about him were shaped in the coming decades—and centuries.

TENSIONS WITHIN EARLY CHRISTIANITY

Internal tensions within the new faith grew out of disagreements about how gentiles could become part of the movement. The very first followers of Jesus were Jews, but if gentiles responded to the gospel message, should they be required, in effect, to become Jews before they could become members of the Christian community? Peter, a close follower of Jesus and a leader in the Jerusalem Christian community, at first insisted that they must become Jews before becoming part of the new community. This no doubt reflected his deep ties to his Jewish traditions. Peter's view, shared by others in the early church, would require such converts to undergo circumcision and observe the dietary laws of Judaism. Paul, on the other hand, contended that in Jesus Christ the original covenant between God and Israel had now been opened up to gentiles and did not require that these gentiles would first have to become

Jews. According to the New Testament documents, a council of leaders in Jerusalem, including Peter, came to agree with Paul's position so that becoming a Jew was not a prerequisite for becoming a member of the growing church. This decision had an immense impact on Christian history.

CHRISTIANITY SEPARATES FROM JUDAISM

Within a century, Christianity became a predominantly gentile movement with a small Jewish Christian minority still within it. By this time it became possible to speak of two religious movements, Christianity and Judaism. Both grew from the same original sources, but each developed its own story. While the seeds of the "two religion" development were in place by the second century of the Christian era, there is clear evidence that Jewish-Christian groups who followed the Law (Torah) were active into at least the third century. These were followers of Jesus but might best be seen as a sect within Judaism and probably reflected beliefs of Jewish Christians before Paul. Even the New Testament Gospel of Matthew can be seen as a reflection of such a group.[11] The existence of these groups, as the Ebionites, was a problem for Christian leaders who eventually labeled them as heretics.

Before the influence of Paul, the early Jerusalem Jewish Christians would have represented the earliest Christian views about Jesus. There is little direct data on what those views might have been before Paul's influence. Jewish scholar Samuel Sandmel wrote, "We can guess at what it was by the process of noting what it was that Paul changed, and by inferring from the changes what it was that was changed."[12] Sandmel concludes that the beliefs of those pre-Pauline Jewish Christians were "a rather usual Judaism to which there were added conceptions about Jesus, but without any accompanying deletions." In short, these early Jerusalem Jewish Christians probably still thought of themselves as within the Jewish faith. They might best be considered to be a sect within Judaism, holding to the Torah but believing that the resurrected Jesus was truly the Messiah of Jewish hope and that he would return in glory to bring in the messianic age.

EARLY CHRISTIAN WRITINGS

The earliest written records of Christian views of Jesus come from the letters of Paul written from about 50 to 57 CE, some twenty years after the crucifixion of Jesus. But Paul's writings give us little information about the life and teachings of Jesus. While Paul's writings were earlier than the New Testament Gospels, the accounts about Jesus given in the first three (synoptic) gospels of the New Testament best reflect what is known about the beliefs of his first followers. Most scholars believe that Mark was the earliest of the four Gospels and was written around the year 70 CE. The Gospels of Matthew and Luke, which were written in the 80s or 90s, apparently used Mark's Gospel as one of their sources.[13] John's Gospel was written later and differs from the synoptic gospels in significant ways.

Since these Gospels were written some forty to sixty years after the crucifixion of Jesus, this time lapse raises the question of just why they were written so long after Jesus's death. Two factors suggest an answer. First, it seems clear that the early Christians were expecting the victorious return of the Messiah Jesus in their own lifetime so there seemed little need for written accounts of the Christian message. The message was passed on orally by various eye-witnesses. Also, many of the main leaders and eyewitnesses of the early church were killed during Nero's persecution of the church in Rome in the mid-60s CE. Given the delay of the return of Jesus and the death of eye-witnesses, it became important to the early church to fix the story in writing.

Another question is also relevant. Given the many years between the time of Jesus's ministry and the writings of these documents, are these documents accurate accounts of Jesus's ministry? Scholars suggest that some of the material in the Gospels were shaped by events and stories that developed *after* Jesus's death. Such material probably reflects not only conflict between early Christians and the Jews who rejected the Christian message but also material designed to defend the new faith and to ground it in words of prophecy and grand events. For example, the stories about the birth of Jesus in Matthew and in Luke, which differ in detail, may not have been in circulation during Jesus's ministry but are probably traditions that developed as the early church formulated its message. While all four Gospels tell of the life and ministry of Jesus, a careful reading shows that each of these documents is written *by* faith *for* faith, and that each carries a story that differs from the others in significant ways. The Gospel writers were creative theologians in their own right.[14]

THE INFLUENCE OF PAUL

In the cluster of voices and opinions in the early Christian movement, Paul's view about Jesus became widely adopted if not always clearly understood. As one New Testament letter puts it, "There are some things in them [Paul's letters] that are hard to understand, which the ignorant and unstable twist to their own destruction." (2 Pet. 3:16) What seems clear is that Paul did not view the message of and about Jesus as a rejection of Judaism. He never used the term "Christian," and he thought of himself as thoroughly Jewish, even when he argued with Peter, James, or others. He viewed his "Christian" message as a development of Judaism, not a rejection of that story.

What Paul does bring into the movement is the view that, in Jesus Christ, God had opened the doors for non-Jews to enter into the faith. Instead of a message meant for Israel alone, Paul introduces a universal story. Paul's view invites a question: What could be the roots of Paul's conviction that God's grace is now open to the entire human community, not limited to the children of Israel and their covenant with God? Concepts, like individuals, do not generally spring from thin air. Paul's universalizing vision appears to run counter to the Judaism in which he was reared. But the Judaism which informed Paul was that of the Hellenistic world where Greek and Roman philosophy had influenced patterns of thought. It seems plausible to suggest that concepts alive in that Hellenistic environment opened Paul up to a more universal invitation to the gospel.

One thought that suggested a more universal view of humanity was that of a basic unity of all existence—a comprehensive "monism." This conviction is reflected in Plato (427?–347 BCE) and Aristotle (384–322 BCE). Aristotle's arguments that God is the first cause of all that is, and that God is also the prime mover of all that moves, suggest such a monism. Plato's followers considered God to be the intelligence that orders the entire universe and that all existence is an emanation from the Divine One. The Stoics taught that the principle of rationality in the cosmos was divine. It appears as though creative human minds seek some way of unifying the wide range of human experience into one unified and intelligible order grounded in one Source.[15]

This human quest for a unified view of reality may also have prompted the demise of polytheism and the move toward monotheism. In the older writings of the Hebrew Bible (Old Testament), the authors assumed there were, in fact, other gods besides the god of Israel. The commandment to "have no other gods before me" reflects this *henotheism*—the belief that other gods exist but that only *your* god should be worshipped. As the Hebrew prophets move down in history, the other gods are finally dismissed as mere fantasy. In Greek religion, the many gods of polytheism shifted somewhat when Zeus is viewed as the major god in the polytheistic system. As the history of speculation moves on, the major god becomes the only god, and other figures are either deleted from reality or are reconstructed as lower spirits or angels. The Greek philosophical mind undercut the mythology of the earlier polytheism. Perhaps the current quest for a Grand Unifying Theory in physics also reflects this urge to discover a rational unity in the nature of things.

Significantly, the Stoics held to a unity of humanity, that all are created equal and that social status is not of consequence. Some proposed that in an ideal age of the past there was neither slavery nor war. The Stoics also believed that human beings, as rational creatures, have the ability to understand the moral order in the cosmos, the law of nature which functions as norms for the laws of human communities.[16] In this Hellenistic setting, speculative winds were blowing in the direction of universalism. Those winds could have nurtured Paul's conviction that God's grace extends to all humankind through Jesus Christ.

As noted earlier, Paul insisted that converts to the new faith did not have to follow the traditions of Judaism, including circumcision and dietary laws, in order to become members of the faith. Crucial to his position is the view that, in Christ, the right relationship with God is now established through faith in the divine act of redemption through the death and victorious resurrection of Jesus. Obedience to the Law (the Torah with its moral and ritual injunctions as interpreted by the Rabbis) is no longer the requirement for this right relationship. In his letter to the Galatians, Paul proclaimed a "freedom that has set us free" from the slavery of obedience to the Law. This rejection of the Law as the means of establishing a right relationship to God is the claim that led to conflict with the Judaism of his day and later Judaism.

The freedom Paul stresses is not, however, to be equated with license. Freedom from Law does not imply lawlessness. Paul's letter to the Romans suggests that some had understood his position to suggest that they might sin all the more so that grace might more abound. (Rom. 6:1 ff.) While Paul sets the Law aside as the *means* of salvation, he does insist that the new life "in Christ" has deep moral implications that he refers to as the "fruit of the Spirit." In his letter to the Galatians, he lists these as "love, joy, peace, patience, kindness, generosity, faithfulness, gentleness, and self-control. There is no law against such things." (Gal. 5:22) He also wrote, "Love does no wrong to a neighbor; therefore, love is the fulfilling of the law." (Rom. 13:10)

Paul's interpretation of the significance of Jesus has left a deep and abiding mark in Christian theology. His views created tensions and divisions in the early Christian community, and these tensions continued to develop with some regularity in Christian history. His significance in this history can be underlined by noting of the twenty-seven documents that make up the New Testament, seven are cited by current scholars as undisputed letters of Paul: Romans, First and Second Corinthians, Galatians, Philippians, First Thessalonians, and Philemon. Historically, seven other New Testament writings have been attributed to Paul: Ephesians, Colossians, Second Thessalonians, First and Second Timothy, Titus, and Hebrews.[17]

The theological fertility of the early Christian centuries produced some followers of Jesus whose views were eventually rejected as heretical by a series of church councils. Some of these views deserve to be reviewed since they illustrate the problem of formulating a new faith in a culture permeated by a plethora of philosophies, sects, and cults. Four will be briefly described: Gnosticism, Docetism, Marcion, and Arius. All four are linked to the question of how Jesus is related to humankind and to God. Was he human? Was he Divine? These are the central questions which *Christology* seeks to answer.

These Christological questions, ironically, were both raised and answered by documents which became part of the New Testament. John's Gospel, written in the late first century or early second century CE, contains names and terms that suggest a deep link between Jesus and God. In Jesus, the divine principle (logos, word) "became flesh and lived among us." (John 1:14) The first chapter in John includes a series of names for Jesus—Son of God, Lamb of God, Son of Man, Messiah, King of Israel. Later in that Gospel, Jesus proclaims, "The Father and I are one." (10:30) "If you know me, you will know my Father also."(14:7) "I am in the Father and the Father is in me."(14:11) John's imagery is rich, but it does not clarify the question of how Jesus is related to God and to humanity.

Paul's letters in the New Testament, written decades before John's Gospel, also include many passages that deal with the figure of Jesus. For Paul, Jesus is the pre-existent Son of God. "For us there is one God, the Father, from whom are all things and for whom we exist, and one Lord, Jesus Christ, through whom are all things and through whom we exist." (1 Cor. 8:6)[18] Regarding the human status of Jesus, Paul writes: "who, though he was in the form of God, did not regard equality with God as something to be exploited, but emptied himself, taking the form of a slave, being born in human likeness. And being found in human form, he humbled himself and became obedient to the point of death—even death on a cross." (Phil. 2:5–8)

The language used by the writer of John's Gospel and by Paul perhaps underlines the question of the relationship between Jesus and God more than it clarifies. Clarification became the task of later church councils. The nature of the issue is reflected in positions taken by groups and individuals who saw themselves as followers of Jesus but were later identified as heretics by developing orthodoxy. These heresies included Gnosticism, Docetism, Marcion, and Arius. These voices sought, as did Paul, to bring the story of Jesus into the Greco-Roman world by linking the message to beliefs and forms of thought alive in that ancient world. They were, in effect, seeking to translate a message rooted in Judaism into Greek.

THE PROBLEM OF THE EXISTENCE OF EVIL

Greek and Roman philosophers had posited a rational and unified theory of all reality, often linking all existence to the One source, the Divine. But there remained a stubborn problem related to this attempt at a grand unity of all things. This was the problem of evil and suffering. For if God, the One, is the ultimate source of all things, why does evil exist? The problem is usually stated as follows: If God is all-good, all-knowing, and all-powerful, then

God's creation should be all-good. But there is evil in the world. Therefore, God cannot be all-good, all-powerful, and all-knowing. Either God allows evil to exist, or God is not able to eradicate evil, or God does not know how to eradicate evil. Greek philosophers had raised this issue, but Christian as well as Jewish thinkers also faced the problem.

There have been a number of attempts to address this persistent issue.[19] One attempt at a solution posited a *dualism* at the heart of reality. This theory suggests that there are two realms of reality, both of which are eternal and uncreated. One is characterized as evil, the other as good. According to this story, the material world is the product of the evil "god." On the other hand, a human soul is a purely spiritual entity from the realm of the Good that has become trapped in a physical body in some way. Suffering and evil, therefore, result from the nature of physical reality and the physical body in which a person finds himself or herself living.

A dualism of this nature was reflected in a Gnostic belief system that appears to have existed by the second century CE. The answer of Gnosticism (having knowledge) to the human situation was to shun the material world, which produces suffering, and to cultivate and embrace the spiritual world. A special knowledge (gnosis) may be reached by an ascetic life that included self-giving philanthropy, poverty, and sexual abstinence. This discipline, along with the quest for wisdom, could lead to emancipation from the human situation. A striking factor in this Gnostic dualism is its repudiation of the material world as basically corrupting and evil. This is in sharp contrast to the pronouncement made at the end of the first creation story in Genesis: "And God saw everything that he had made, and indeed, it was very good." (Gen. 1:31) Some suggest that the ascetic streak in Christianity, in contrast to Judaism, reflects a remnant of this ancient dualism.

SOME HERETICS: MARCION, ARIUS, DOCETICS

A leader in the early Christian community created dissension by holding views similar to that of the Gnostics. This man was Marcion (85–160 CE).[20] After studying both Old Testament and early Christian writings, Marcion came to the conclusion that there must be two Gods since the activities of the God of the Old Testament were in sharp contrast to the God proclaimed by Jesus. Interpreting the Genesis creation story literally, Marcion noted that this God must have had a physical body because he was recorded as walking in the Garden of Eden. Furthermore, this God surely could not be all-knowing since he had to search for Adam and Eve in the Garden. Marcion deemed the Old Testament God as a tyrant and that the true God to be worshipped was the Father of Jesus Christ. This dualistic view of an evil God and also a good God was not uncommon in the ancient world. Marcion concluded that the Genesis creator God was inferior to the Father of Jesus.

Marcion was instrumental in the process that eventually led the Church to select twenty-seven books as the New Testament canon of scripture. In Marcion's day, the New Testament canon had not yet been formulated by the Church. To help guide his followers, Marcion selected a group of documents that he deemed as the authoritative writings for the faith. He included much of the Gospel of Luke and also ten letters of Paul—but no other writings. He rejected entirely the religious authority of the Old Testament and severed Christianity from Judaism. Marcion did believe that Jesus was the Savior sent from God, and he considered Paul's theology to be the norm for the faith.

While Marcion had a following in the early church, Christian leaders eventually rejected his view of two distinct Gods and his repudiation of Judaism and the Old Testament scriptures. In spurning Marcion, the Christian community retained the Old Testament as scripture and Judaism as part of God's redeeming work. Marcion's attempt to establish an authoritative set of writings as scripture forced the Christian community to make distinctions among the great variety of writings circulating at the time. Eventually, this led to the selection of the twenty-seven writings that now make up the New Testament.

If Marcion's influence made it necessary for the Church to select an authoritative set of writings, the New Testament, then Arius (ca. 250–336 CE) made it necessary for Christian leaders to make a decision about the relation of Jesus to God and to humanity. While Arius believed that Jesus was the Son of God, he did not believe that Jesus had always existed but was, instead, a created being. As the Son of God, Arius argued, Jesus was distinct from God and subordinate to God. A passage from the Gospel of John suggested this view: "If you loved me, you would rejoice that I am going to the Father, because the Father is greater than I." (John 14:28) Evidently those deemed as heretics could also quote scripture. The Ecumenical Council of Nicaea (325 CE) declared Arian's views to be heretical.

While Arius held that Jesus was less than God the Father, other early Christians argued that Jesus was not a truly *human* being. These were the *Docetics*, named from a Greek word that meant "to seem." They asserted that Jesus *was* truly divine. Since he was truly divine, it follows that he could not have had a physical body, could not have suffered, and certainly could not have been killed. Hence, he could not have been truly a human being.

Some Docetics held that Jesus only appeared (seemed) to be a man of flesh and blood, but he was not. His body was an illusion. Others thought that Jesus was truly a man in the flesh, but when a dove descended on Jesus at his baptism, another entity called Christ entered his body and enabled him to perform miracles. This entity abandoned Jesus when he went to the cross.

Since Jesus was divine, according to Docetics and Gnostics, he could not die. Therefore, he could not have been crucified. Instead, when Jesus stumbled while carrying his cross, some Docetics proposed that Simon of Cyrene was brought in to carry the cross for Jesus. At that point, Jesus escaped and the Romans, by mistake, crucified Simon instead of Jesus. This view appears to be reflected in some passages in the Muslim holy book, the Quran.

CONSTANTINE AND CHURCH COUNCILS

These disputes about the relationship of Jesus to God the Father became a concern for Emperor Constantine, who desired unity in a religion that was to help bind together his empire. Thus the First Council of Nicaea was called by Constantine in 325 CE. This Council helped achieve unity by asserting that "Jesus Christ, [was] the Son of God, begotten of the Father . . . Light of Light, very God of very God, begotten, not made, being of one substance with the Father." The Nicene Creed solidly established the relationship of Jesus with God but did not clarify the question of Jesus's human status. This matter was clarified by the Council of Chalcedon (451 CE), which declared: "Our Lord Jesus Christ, [is] the same perfect in Godhead and also perfect in manhood; truly God and truly man." The determinations of these two Councils have been accepted widely by the Eastern Orthodox Church, the Roman Catholic Church, and the major Protestant reformers, Luther and Calvin.

The contentions and wrangling involved in these Ecumenical Councils may appear to many moderns as theological hairsplitting. But behind or within the technical language and the seeming paradox of the truly God and truly Man declaration some basic issues were at stake. The Councils decided, in effect, that Jesus Christ was to be understood as both *adequate* and *relevant*. In order for his life, death, crucifixion, and resurrection to be adequate to the task of redeeming humankind, Jesus Christ must be truly divine. But if his life and teachings were to be relevant to human beings, he must also be truly human. In Christian history, there has been a temptation to argue that since Jesus Christ was divine, he cannot serve as a role model for his followers. The creeds undercut that view by maintaining that he was, indeed, truly human.

THE INFLUENCE OF AUGUSTINE

After the formation of these basic creeds, ensuing Christian history often tended to emphasize either the divine or the human nature of Jesus Christ. Emphasis on the divine nature was linked to a diagnosis of the human situation that was sufficiently grim to warrant the need for the redeeming work of God. In 354 CE, a child born in Africa of a pagan father and a Christian mother became a man whose writings reflected just such a grim picture. As one of the most influential philosophical theologians in Christian history, he became known as St. Augustine.[21] After flirting with Manichaeism, which reflected Gnostic dualism, he was later influenced by Neo-Platonic thought. In 387 CE, he converted to Christianity and was baptized. "Augustine's most important contribution to the history of human psychology came in his doctrine of sin, his investigation . . . of what made Christ necessary . . . of the misery rather than of the grandeur of humanity."[22] In his analysis, Augustine sought "to gauge the magnitude of the human crime by first taking the measure of the one on whom the divine punishment of the cross had been imposed and thus . . . making the diagnosis fit the prescription."[23] This perspective was developed in his *Confessions* wherein he reflected on, among other topics, the hedonistic lifestyle shared with friends during his early years. In commenting on some episodes from his early years, Augustine realized that the young man he now recalled found joy in his actions precisely because he knew such actions were wrong. He had loved evil rather than the good.

In his reflections on the nature of sin, Augustine came to believe that there are some aspects of the human experience that are so fundamentally threatening that we are unable to recognize the depth of the problem until we have some possible solution. For him, the light of Christ revealed to him not only the gift of forgiving divine love, but it also enabled him to see the depth of his own brokenness. The solution made it possible to see the problem. Without the solution, the depth of the problem cannot be endured.

Augustine is probably best known for his development of the doctrine of original sin, which maintains that the sin of Adam and Eve is inherited by all descendents of this first couple. As New England Puritan primers later taught, "In Adam's fall we sinned all." Although Augustine held that Biblical texts should be interpreted metaphorically if a literal interpretation would appear to clash either with science or God-given reason, he evidently took the Genesis story of creation and of Adam and Eve quite literally. This inherited sin results in a corruption of the passions of both the soul and the body, greatly weakening the freedom of the will.

Original Sin also makes divine grace *necessary* for salvation. Because of The Fall and its consequences, no human being is able to acquire salvation in any other way. Just how that grace is made available becomes a point of dispute in Christian history. For traditional Roman Catholicism, this grace is mediated through the sacraments of the Church, seen as the body of Christ. In the thought of the two major reformers, Martin Luther and John Calvin, this saving grace is a free gift through faith (trust) and is not mediated through a priest or a church. Faith, itself, is also a gift. But for Augustine and most Christians after him, the required grace derives solely from the work of redemption through Jesus Christ. This grace frees the Christian from a type of bondage to sin and enables a life active in love for others. In his commentary on 1 John 4:4–12, Augustine provides what is, perhaps, the shortest moral rule ever given: "Love and do what you will."

THE CHALLENGE OF PELAGIUS TO AUGUSTINE

While Augustine's view of sin and redemption has been deeply influential in Christian history, not all who thought of themselves as Christian shared Augustine's generally pessimistic view of human nature. A dissenting voice came through a British-born monk with an ascetic orientation, Pelagius (fl. 390–418 CE). Pelagius rejected the doctrine of original sin and expressed a strong doctrine of freewill. As a practicing ascetic, he evidently was not plagued by the moral tensions experienced by Augustine. Here, too, a theological answer may reflect the nature of the problem to be solved. Without a deep sense of guilt and sin, grace loses its significance.

Reflecting the influence of Greek thought, Pelagius held that human beings are rational creatures with an essential freedom of thought and decision. The sin of Adam belongs only to Adam, not to the human race. An individual must sin in order to be a sinner. As a morally responsible entity, the person must have the freedom and ability to abide by moral law. Moral law without such freedom would be a contradiction in terms. In Kant's later phrasing, "ought" implies "can." Pelagius was accused by Augustinians of denying the need of grace in order to follow divine law.

In contrast to Augustine, Pelagius appeared to argue that a person is quite capable of following divine law without the aid of forgiving and empowering divine grace. This view would tend to undercut the significance of the Church as an instrument through which grace is administered. Pelagius was declared a heretic by the Council of Carthage (418 CE), which upheld Augustine's views. This conflict between Augustine and Pelagius was of major significance and tends to be repeated often in church history.

ATONEMENT THEORIES

If salvation requires the forgiveness of sin, original or personal, a need arose to clarify just how the work of Jesus attained that end. New Testament documents, especially the letters of Paul, speak of the redeeming work of Jesus Christ through his crucifixion and resurrection, yet none of them provided a clarification of just how the crucifixion and resurrection achieved that end. The need to clarify this issue led to the development of various theories of atonement which sought to explain how Jesus brought about reconciliation (at-one-ment) between God and humankind. Paul had written about the "wisdom of the cross" which was "a stumbling block to Jews and foolishness to the Gentiles." (1 Cor. 1:18ff.) Later Christians sought to clarify the nature of that "wisdom." While there is no official Christian dogma of the atonement, two theories have been influential: Anselm's *satisfaction* theory and Abelard's *moral influence* theory.

ANSELM'S SATISFACTION THEORY

Anselm (1033–1109 CE), Bishop of Canterbury, developed a view of the atonement in his dialogue *Cur Deus Homo* (Why God Was A Man). His theory reflects the Old Testament tradition of the forgiveness of sins through appropriate sacrifice. It also reflects the words of John the Baptist regarding Jesus: "Here is the Lamb of God who takes away the sin of the world." (John 1:29) Couched in legal theory of his own time, Anselm argued that the severity of an offense, and the justice due, is related to the rank of the one against whom the offense is committed. An offense against a king was greater than a crime against a commoner. The fall of mankind through the sin of Adam and Eve was an offense against an infinite God and, therefore, represented an infinite offense. Furthermore, justice requires that the penalty for an offense must equal the magnitude of the offense itself. The sin against God by Adam and Eve required an infinite penalty, and no mere human being could supply such. Therefore, the only possible source able to pay such a penalty was God. But since the offense was committed by man, the requirement of justice is that man must provide the recompense.

Anselm concluded that Jesus Christ was not only wholly God but also wholly man; therefore, in the divine sacrifice of the death of Christ on the cross, the two requirements of justice were accomplished. Anselm's theory sought to demonstrate that God is perfectly just since genuine guilt received its due penalty. Anselm also sought to show that God is perfectly merciful in that divine love paid the penalty and redeems mankind. In acknowledging this redeeming love, the person of faith finds forgiveness and is also enabled to live a life reflecting such love.[24] Anselm's theory never became a dogma in the church and there were other competing theories of atonement. Perhaps his theory became widely accepted because it reflects the intuition that a price must be paid for guilt—a common theme in systems of justice and law. Thus since human beings are unable to pay an adequate price, God must do so.

ABELARD'S MORAL INFLUENCE THEORY

Another theory of atonement moved away from the legal bargaining that was emphasized in Anselm's theory. Instead, it stressed the love reflected in the self-sacrificing act of Christ. This view was presented by the French philosopher/theologian, Pierre Abelard (1079–1142 CE), often cited as a man of genius. Jaroslav Pelikan summarizes Abelard's view:

> The purpose of the cross . . . was to bring about a change in sinners, to thaw their frozen hearts with the warmth and sunshine of divine love. Christ did not die on the cross to change the mind of God . . . but to "reveal the love [of God] to us or to convince us how much we ought to love him 'who did not spare even his own Son' for us." True love was self-sacrificing love, and God had demonstrated it uniquely by giving up his own Son to the death of the cross. This exhibited the authentic nature of love and the depth of divine love, thus making human love, even self-sacrificing human love, possible.[25]

STRAYING FROM ORTHODOXY

The contrasting theories of Anselm and Abelard anticipate differing views about Jesus expressed by Christians in the coming centuries. Some will emphasize the sinful nature of mankind and the need for the saving grace of God in Christ, while others will focus on the life and death of Jesus as a model for the Christian life. Some emphasize the divinity of Jesus, others the humanity of Jesus, and some will deny the divinity of Jesus altogether. These divisions among the followers of Jesus should come as no surprise since such tensions were present in the early years of the Jesus movement.

The differing views of Jesus expressed after the Middle Ages resulted from a variety of influences and challenges. The Protestant Reformation of the sixteenth century weakened the power of the Roman Catholic Church and opened the door for the expression of views about Jesus and Christian doctrine that challenged various orthodoxies. Both the Church of Rome and ruling monarchs found it increasingly difficult to enforce conformity in matters of faith. Heresy was still a dangerous venture, but as history moved on, the zeal for burning heretics waned. Reformation leaders Martin Luther and John Calvin challenged the authority of the Roman Catholic Church. The basis for their Protestant Reformation faith was the sole authority of scripture. Instead of the word becoming flesh (John 1:14), the word became words. A focus developed on Biblical authority as the revealed word of God without error. This shifted the emphasis from the figure of Jesus to the Bible itself and set the stage for challenges to a variety of traditional views during the Enlightenment.

The Enlightenment of the eighteenth century changed the religious scene. By that time European peoples had long wearied of wars of religion and the persecution of dissident persons and groups. The absolute monarchies and the hardened dogmas of the Roman Catholic Church were called into question. Reason and scientific method were stressed. A demand for individual liberty and freedom of conscience developed.

The emphasis on reason began to weaken the belief that the Bible was divinely inspired and without error. Emerging Biblical scholarship also began to erode the authority of scripture. This erosion was reflected in doubts raised about the authorship of the Torah (the first five books of the Old Testament), sometimes referred to as the "books of Moses." A long tradition held that Moses was the author of those books. But as early as the seventeenth century, Baruch Spinoza (1632–1677 CE), a Jewish philosopher, pointed out that Moses could not have written *all* of the Torah since the final verses tell of his death and burial. (Deut. 34:5 f.) Such questioning of traditional views threatened to become a slippery slope that unnerved many believers. The slope turned into a precipice for some believers in the nineteenth and twentieth centuries when Biblical scholarship detected the marks of human fingerprints in the origins of scripture.

While the Enlightenment and emerging science brought challenges to the Roman Catholic and Eastern Orthodox communities, these churches have adjusted to such challenges while holding largely to the formulations of the early creeds.[26] For conservative Protestants, the central message has been that of forgiveness and salvation through Christ. This conservative message was reflected in the work of evangelists such as Dwight L. Moody, Billy Sunday, and Billy Graham. Some conservatives—Roman Catholic and Protestant—have often fiercely resisted some aspects of modern science, such as the theory of evolution, since such theories contradict a literal reading of some passages of scripture.[27]

THE WIDENING SPECTRUM

The Protestant spectrum, however, has produced other less orthodox views about Jesus as a variety of churches and sects developed over the centuries. This variety is best explained by noting that in Protestantism there is no single Church authority, as in the Papacy of the Roman Catholic Church, which can provide a firm hand on matters of faith and morals. Given that the Bible became the central authority for Protestants, it seemed inevitable that there would develop many disagreements about what the Bible actually teaches. The scriptures may be infallible, but fallible persons do the interpreting. Furthermore, in Protestantism there is no mediating church or priest between the believer and his or her God. The believer stands alone in the immediate presence of the divine and responds as an individual. Such convictions brought with them a sense of freedom of conscience and religious liberty. This cluster of factors contributed to the variety of voices emerging in the Protestant spectrum. Since all such voices cannot be traced in a work of this scope, only a few that represent major shifts from more orthodox expressions of the Christian faith will be noted here.

UNITARIANS

While Unitarians have never been great in number, they reflect a major reconstruction of the Christian story brought about by challenges such as the emphasis on reason and the role of science. This movement gets its name from the conviction that God is a single entity in contrast to the traditional view of the triune nature of God as a trinity of the Father, the Son, and the Holy Spirit. Scientist and theologian Michael Servetus (1511–1553 CE) expressed such a view in his book *The Errors of the Trinity*. He was raised as a Catholic child in Spain, but explored the reformation views of Martin Luther and John Calvin after experiencing outrage at the pomp and luxury of the Pope and his supporters. His study of the Bible led him to conclude that the doctrine of the Trinity had no basis in scriptures but resulted from the intrusion of Greek philosophy into matters theological.

While denying the Trinity, Servetus viewed Jesus as the Son of the Eternal God and born of the Virgin Mary. His denial of the Trinity, however, was seen as a dangerous heresy in both Roman Catholic and Protestant circles. While Servetus escaped from Roman Catholic authorities, he was later arrested in Calvin's Geneva, brought to trial, and burned at the stake. His dying words are reported to be, "Jesus, Son of the Eternal God, have mercy on me." Some sources add "and on all humanity." Servetus was not a Unitarian in seventeenth century or contemporary terms, but his death brought strong negative reactions in Europe and resulted in the spread of his writings and theology. Contemporary Unitarians see him as something like a patron saint.

Another early figure in the Unitarian mode was the Englishman John Biddle (1615–1662), considered by some as the father of English Unitarianism. He held that the Bible was the Word of God and accepted the doctrine of the Virgin Birth, but he rejected the doctrine of the Trinity by denying the pre-existence of Christ. He also rejected original sin and predestination. Both doctrines are rooted in the works of St. Augustine and affirmed by St. Thomas Aquinas and the Protestant Reformers John Calvin and Martin Luther. Biddle also denied eternal punishment of unredeemed sinners, a position later affirmed by the Universalists and others. Given the temper of the times, Biddle raised the ire of many and was imprisoned by a hostile English Parliament a number of times under the Blasphemy Act. But the desire to destroy heretics by burning, drowning, or beheading had receded in England by the seventeenth century, and Biddle was not put to death. He finally died in prison.

GEORGE FOX AND THE QUAKERS

Another small but influential community of believers, the Quakers, was founded in England by George Fox (1624–1691). A devoutly religious man, Fox started on a quest for religious answers at the age of nineteen. He found no adequate answers in the spectrum of religious alternatives of his day. His quest resulted in what he experienced as a call from God directing him to Jesus, who could speak to his needs. A line from one of the gospels provided a basic theme for Fox in its declaration that Jesus was "The true light, which enlightens everyone." (John 1:9) Fox took this to mean that each person has an inner light that enables him or her to interpret the Word of God and to openly express convictions about spiritual matters. This basic belief implied that no church or priest is required since each individual has his or her own capacity to find the truth needed for the life of faith. This inner light also implied a thoroughly egalitarian view in that all persons are of equal worth, be they male, female, slave, or free.

For Fox, simplicity in religion was also central with no need for ceremonies, gowns, creeds and other forms of worship that struck Fox as empty of religious significance. His followers were taught to worship in silence, but they could speak when they felt so moved by the Holy Spirit. Later, they became known as the Friends since they thought of themselves as friends of Jesus. Present day Quakers will show their concern for others by holding them "in the light." Pennsylvania, the colony founded by the Quaker William Penn with a land charter from King Charles II, became a colony that honored religious freedom. The Quakers also became active in the movement to abolish slavery and generally opposed all types of warfare. For the Quakers, Jesus is seen largely as a divine and loving friend who can lead them safely through the human journey.

GROWING TOLERATION

The violent repression of heretical voices which took place in the sixteenth century gradually subsided. The English Act of Toleration (1689 CE), reflected a less hostile attitude toward dissident and helped to clear the way for alternative views. The Unitarian and Quaker followers of Jesus were symptomatic of the proliferation of Protestant groups within England in the seventeenth century. Some that have survived into the twenty-first century include Presbyterians, Congregationalists, Baptists, and Unitarians. The Familists, Ranters, Seekers, and Fifth Monarchy Men have faded from history. Exactly one century after the English Act of Toleration, the full legal expression of religious freedom became part of the Constitution of the United States. Twelve amendments to the Constitution were proposed to state legislatures by Congress in 1789. Ten of the twelve eventually became the Bill of Rights. The First Amendment asserts: "Congress shall make no law respecting an establishment of religion, or prohibiting the free exercise thereof."

In many nations, the followers of Jesus now had a range of choices in their search for an answer to basic religious needs. Since perceived religious needs can vary widely, religious answers to such needs will also vary. The description of Augustine's view of Jesus earlier in this chapter included the suggestion that there is a correlation between the diagnosis of the religious *problem* and the prescribed religious *answer*. Augustine's view of the religious prescription (Jesus as the divine redeemer) correlated to the grim diagnosis of the sinful nature of humankind. If sin is emphasized, so also is divine grace. A similar correlation seems to appear during and after the Enlightenment. The divine status of Jesus is lowered, if not removed altogether, in the rejection of the doctrine of the Trinity. This relative loss of divine status relates to a different role for Jesus among such followers. Instead of being a redeemer from sin, Jesus becomes a model for human behavior. This also involves less emphasis on guilt. Jesus is a guide, not a stern judge or Savior from sin. The Enlightenment figure of Thomas Jefferson reflects this transition from Jesus as Savior to Jesus as moral compass.

THOMAS JEFFERSON

It seems fitting to close this chapter with a figure who reflects the Enlightenment mindset and whose views would, for some, exempt him from the label of "Christian." This figure is Thomas Jefferson (1743–1826). Even though his beliefs strayed far from traditional Christianity, he never renounced his relationship with the Anglican Church into which he was born and which was the established church of Virginia in his day. While his status as Christian could be debated, he could be included in a large tent definition of "Christian" as "a person who holds Jesus as the central factor of his or her religious faith and life." As a typical Enlightenment figure, Jefferson was evidently not plagued by the deep sense of sinfulness reflected in St. Augustine. Jefferson's religious quest and need was not for a means of lifting the weight of sin from his soul but for finding a moral pathway in his life ventures. He found in Jesus an answer for this need.

Jefferson, reflecting the views of his British Unitarian friend Joseph Priestley, was convinced that many who thought of themselves as followers of Jesus had perverted his teachings and blurred them with needless mysticisms and subtleties. "Jefferson's list of these corruptions was long, extending to such as original sin, the virgin birth, the atonement, predestination, salvation by faith, transubstantiation, bodily resurrection, and above all the

Trinity." Jefferson also held that "miracles were an affront to the demands of reason and the laws of nature, and Jesus had performed not a one."[28]

On the other hand, Jefferson spoke of Jesus the man with high praise and considered his moral teachings to be the best that have ever been taught by a human being. Jefferson also reflected some traditional beliefs, such as the existence of God and an afterlife. It is not clear that he was among the Deists who held that while God created the universe, that God allows the world to run its own course and does not intervene directly into human affairs. While Jefferson apparently believed in an afterlife that involved meeting again those whom he had loved and worked with during his lifetime, there seems to be no clear evidence that he believed in some kind of Hell or eternal punishment. His rejection of stern Calvinism suggests that he might have shared the views of the Universalists of his day who rejected the idea of an eternal Hell.

Jefferson's religious convictions were forcefully reflected in what has become known as "Jefferson's Bible." Intent on reducing Christian faith to its basics and removing irrational elements, he proceeded with scissors and paste to severely edit the New Testament documents. He omitted anything that represented supernatural events, such as the virgin birth, the resurrection, and miracles. He included what he deemed as the true sayings of Jesus and some of his actions. Nothing else in the New Testament, aside from selected portions of the Gospels, was included. The focus was entirely on Jesus and his teachings. The resulting "Bible" was quite short. It begins with the account of Caesar's decree of taxation and ends with the burial of Jesus when a stone was laid at the door of the tomb and the disciples departed. Reflecting Jefferson's own abilities, he presented the chosen passages in Greek, Latin, French, and English. A copy of Jefferson's "Bible," entitled *The Life and Morals of Jesus of Nazareth*, was published by the U.S. Congress in 1904 and can be found in the Smithsonian Institution in Washington, DC.[29]

Closing this account of "Jesus in Christianity" with the views of Thomas Jefferson does not imply that he has the last word. The Christian story is still told around the world in a variety of voices, churches, and sects. Roman Catholics, Eastern Orthodox, and most Protestants still affirm the early Christians creeds. The influence of St. Augustine is deeply implanted in both Roman Catholicism and the Protestantism of Martin Luther and John Calvin. For all such Christians, Jesus is primarily a Savior. The official Roman Catholic Catechism carries a nuanced version of a very traditional view.[30] The largest Protestant denomination in the United States, the Southern Baptist Convention, holds to the Trinity, the Virgin Birth, a sinless Jesus, substitutionary atonement, Jesus's resurrection and his victorious return.[31] These Baptists also hold to the view that human salvation comes through Jesus only.[32] Many continue to claim him as Savior and Lord in strongly traditional terms while others find in him a model for a truly human life. In this way,

Jesus is still seen by many as both truly human and truly divine—thereby underlining the greatness of a Great Man.

NOTES

1. For works that explore the Christian story in detail, see Roland Bainton, *Christianity* (Boston: Houghton Mifflin, 2000), and Jaroslav Pelikan, *Jesus Through the Centuries: His Place in the History of Culture* (New Haven: Yale University Press, 1985).

2. *Merriam-Webster's Collegiate Dictionary* (Springfield, Massachusetts: Merriam-Webster, Incorporated, Eleventh Edition, 2014).

3. The term "Christianity" as a designation for this new faith did not appear until almost a century after the death of Jesus. Therefore, the early years of the faith might best be described as the "Jesus Movement." But for the sake of clarity and consistency the term "Christian" will be used to designate the movement from its beginning. See L. Michael White, *From Jesus to Christianity* (New York: Harper Collins, 2004), 117 f.

4. Works dealing with the life and teachings of Jesus would include Raymond Brown, *An Introduction to the New Testament* (New York: Doubleday, 1997); Delbert Burkett, *An Introduction to the New Testament and the Origins of Christianity* (Cambridge, UK: Cambridge University Press, 2001); and Bart Ehrman, *The New Testament: A Historical Introduction to the Early Christian Writings* (Oxford: Oxford University Press, 2008).

5. For helpful descriptions of this religious setting, see White, chapters two through four, and Rodney Stark, *The Triumph of Christianity* (New York: Harper Collins, 2011), chapters one and two.

6. For a probing analysis of the problem of death, see Ernest Becker, *The Denial of Death* (New York: The Free Press, 1973).

7. See Rodney Stark, *Discovering God: The Origins of the Great Religions and the Evolution of Belief* (New York: Harper Collins, 2007), chapter 3, for a sociological analysis of religions as competitors in a marketplace.

8. Did Paul have this cult in mind when writing Galatians 5:12?

9. White, 219.

10. Paula Fredriksen, *From Jesus to Christ* (New Haven and London: Yale University Press, second edition, 2000), 212.

11. John Gager, *Who Made Early Christianity? The Jewish Lives of the Apostle Paul* (New York: Columbia University Press, 2015), 94. See chapter 4 for development. See, also, White 243–247 on Matthew's Gospel.

12. Samuel Sandmel, *We Jews and Jesus* (Woodstock, VT: First SkyLight Paths, 2000), 115. Fredriksen agrees, 212.

13. For the "synoptic problem," see Pheme Perkins, *Introduction to the Synoptic Gospels* (Grand Rapids, Michigan: Wm. B Eerdmans Publishing Co. 2007), and White 105 ff.

14. See Fredriksen, 18–61, for an analysis of the similarities and differences among the Gospels.

15. For the influence of Greek philosophy on a developing monotheism, see Robert Wright, *The Evolution of God* (New York: Little, Brown and Company, 2009), 182 f.

16. For a description of this Hellenistic setting, see Bainton, 21 ff., and Fredriksen, 9–17. This Hellenistic influence is also reflected in the Gospel of John. "In the beginning was the Word [Greek, *Logos*], and the Word was with God, and the Word was God." (John 1:1) The Greek word "logos" carries a weight of meaning that no English word can capture.

17. See White, 143–168.

18. This thought is reflected in a passage from the Book of Acts 17:28 which has Paul saying, "For 'in him we live and move and have our being'; as even some of your poets have said." The passage Paul cites is attributed to Epimenides, a seventh or sixth century BCE Greek poet. This, again, reflects Paul's Hellenistic background.

19. Plato, for instance, suggested in his Socratic dialogue, *Timaeus*, that the material world we experience was put together by a demiurge (craftsman, artisan, and not a high God) who had

a fine blueprint for creation (Plato's famous "forms" or "ideas"), but the material he had to work with was woefully inferior. Therefore, while the demiurge did the best he could, the final product has many failings because of the faulty material he had available. From thence comes evil. Plato taught that the physical body is a "prison house" of the soul, and that, at death, the soul is released from this prison and can return to its all-good origins.

20. See White, 408 f.
21. Augustine's impact on Christianity and western culture has been extensive. See Peter Brown, *St. Augustine of Hippo* (Berkeley: University of California Press, 1967). For a highly rated work on Augustine's view of love, see Hannah Arendt, *Love and St. Augustine*, Joanna Scott and Judith Stark, eds. (Chicago: University of Chicago Press, 1996).
22. Pelikan, 185.
23. Ibid., 72.
24. Ibid., 107 f. for a development of Anselm's theory.
25. Ibid., 106.
26. See *Catechism of the Catholic Church* (New York: Doubleday, 1995) for a full development of official Roman Catholic teaching. There is, however, a good deal of ferment within the church.
27. See George Marsden, *Understanding Fundamentalism and Evangelicalism* (Grand Rapids, Michigan: William Eerdmans, 1991), and Ronald Numbers, *The Creationists: From Scientific Creationism to Intelligent Design* (Berkeley and Los Angeles, California: University of California Press, 1993).
28. Prothero, 22–23.
29. For an overview of Jefferson's convictions, see Prothero, 19–32, and Jon Meacham, *American Gospel: God, the Founding Fathers, and the Making of a Nation* (New York: Random House, 2007).
30. *Catechism of the Catholic Church*, 1995.
31. See *Resolution On Southern Baptists And Roman Catholics*, 1994. Orlando, Florida.
32. This issue will be explored in chapter seven.

Chapter Three

Jesus in Judaism

Jesus of Nazareth was a Jew. Yet some followers of the religion that grew from his life and teachings have, for centuries, expressed contempt for Judaism.[1] Similarly, voices within Judaism have countered with equally disdainful attacks on Christianity. Such hostility may be explained as the result of competing religious stories. The stories of one faith challenged the very foundation of the other faith. The competition between Judaism and Christianity may be seen as a type of sibling rivalry since both are rooted in the Hebrew Bible (Old Testament). Or the challenge may be seen as that of an offspring—Christianity—that seeks to subvert and replace the mother—Judaism. In the past century, there has been a noticeable move from mutual disdain and condescension to tolerance, and even to respectful acceptance.

Since Judaism had roots some centuries before the advent of Christianity, this new faith came onto the scene as a challenge to the older. A number of alternative responses by Jewish voices to this challenge were possible. One response was to defeat the opponent by attacking the moral credibility of its messenger, Jesus. Another was to show that the opposing view must be false in terms of beliefs already solidly in place; tradition trumps. Still another response was to embrace the new messenger (Jesus) and claim him as one of their own. The latter approach separated Jesus from Christianity while also rejecting the "pagan" doctrines that had grown up around him. All three responses eventually developed. A review of the main features of the Judaism of Jesus's day will help to clarify Jewish responses to the Christian message.

THE SHAPING OF JUDAISM

While the story of the people of Israel is traced back to the very beginnings in the Hebrew Bible, also known as the Old Testament, the shaping of the religion called Judaism takes place after several monumental historical events.[2] One of these events took place when the Babylonians crushed the Kingdom of Judah and destroyed the Jerusalem Temple in 586 BCE. This also resulted in the Babylonian Exile when many Jews were forced from their homeland by the conquerors and resettled in Babylon. Another significant event took place near the end of the same century when the Zoroastrian Persians, under Cyrus, conquered Babylon. Cyrus gave the Jews permission to return to their homeland. At first only a small number returned since many had established a life and a community in Babylon.

Later, around 450 BCE, a Persian ruler allowed Nehemiah, Ezra, and others to return to Jerusalem. With support from the Persians (Zoroastrians) Nehemiah and Ezra worked to rebuild the Jerusalem Temple and to set up a form of Jewish government. It was during the Exile and the years after the return to Jerusalem that the final compilation of the Torah—the Pentateuch or the first five books of the Old Testament—was carried out. Judaism was taking shape as a people of the book. The Torah, interpreted over the centuries to come, became central to the faith. The events of the Babylonian Exile shaped the story of the people of Israel into one of exile and return that has become a characteristic theme in Judaism.[3]

REVOLTS AGAINST THE ROMAN EMPIRE

In the centuries after the return from the Exile, Jews lost control of their region to the Greeks under Alexander the Great and later to the Romans when that empire dominated the Mediterranean areas. The tyranny of the Roman rule resulted in a variety of individuals and groups intent on driving out the Romans. Among these voices were a number who either claimed to be the promised Messiah or were looked upon as such. Such a Messiah was expected to lead the Jews to victory, through God's power, over the enemy and restore the Kingdom. Two disastrous conflicts took place as a result of Jewish revolts against Roman rule in 70 CE and 135 CE.[4] In the first conflict, the Romans took four years to clear the rebellion in the countryside. Then, after a siege of six months, the Roman legions under Titus breached the walls defending Jerusalem, torched the city, destroyed the Temple, and slaughtered many. A second conflict that took place some sixty-five years later, grew out of a claim to Messiahship by a Simon Bar Kokhba. Once again, Roman legions crushed the revolt, slaughtered thousands, enslaved great numbers, and laid waste to much of the region. While under the heel of Rome, Jews were not allowed into Jerusalem except for a day of mourning that commemorated the destruction of the first and second Temple. These events effectively erased Jewish control over their homeland in that ancient world and contributed to the *diaspora*—the dispersion of Jews out of their homeland into other nations and lands.[5]

DIVISIONS WITHIN JUDAISM

By the time of the Christian era, there were a number of divisions within Judaism, usually identified as the Sadducees, the Pharisees, the Essenes, and the Zealots. The Sadducees were the elitists who worked most closely with Roman rule and also controlled the rituals of the Jerusalem Temple. To a point, they were willing to incorporate elements of Hellenism (Greek) into their lives, but they accepted only the written Law (Torah) as authoritative and insisted on its literal interpretation. They did not believe in life beyond the death of the body and the related idea of God's judgment on the other side of death.

The Pharisees—led by Rabbis—turned out to be the most important group since they became the spiritual fathers of modern Judaism. They believed in an Oral Law—legal commentary on the Torah—that supplemented the Torah or written law. This Oral Law eventually becomes fixed mainly in the Babylonian Talmud by 600 CE. The Pharisees were the liberals of their day and believed in an after-life that involved God's punishment of the wicked and rewards for the righteous. They also believed in the coming of the Messiah. While New Testament documents reflect elements of hostility between Jesus and the Pharisees, he had more in common with that group than any other Jewish group at the time.

The Essenes believed Jerusalem and the Temple had become corrupted. As a remedy, the Essenes moved into a desert community and lived by a set of strict rules as they awaited the coming of the Messiah. The Essenes are generally believed to be the authors of the famous Dead Sea scrolls discovered in 1947. When the Essenes resisted the Roman army that marched on Jerusalem in 66 CE, they were evidently erased from history. They may have anticipated that God would intervene on their behalf against the Roman Legions.

Characterized by their zeal for the Jewish nation, the Zealots represented a group that plotted forceful action to drive out the Romans. These Zealots were probably largely responsible for the disastrous revolts against Rome.

With the destruction of the Jerusalem Temple, the role of the priest in Judaism was essentially removed along with the party of the Sadducees. The leadership of this community of faith now fell to the rabbis, largely members of the Pharisees. Temple sacrifice was no longer possible. The Torah became the central focus of the faith. While he was crucified some decades before the destruction of the Jerusalem Temple, Jesus of Nazareth (ca.4 BCE–ca. 30 CE) lived during this tumultuous period of his people.

EARLY WRITTEN REFERENCES TO JESUS

References to Jesus from Jewish sources were slow in developing. The New Testament Gospels, written some thirty-five to eighty years after the death of Jesus, assert that Jesus had a sizeable popular following—as well as opponents—during his lifetime. But the lack of other sources suggests that Jesus was a marginal figure in Palestine during his lifetime and for some decades following. His brief ministry that ended in his crucifixion was minor news in a land dominated by a cruel empire. *Antiquities* (93 CE), by the Jewish historian, Flavius Josephus, contains two references to Jesus, but these references show the mark of later Christian reworking since the comments reflect a clearly Christian view of Jesus. The first writings that carry any significant details about Jesus were the Christian Gospels.

THE CHRISTIAN GOSPELS

The Christian Gospels—documents clearly written *by* faith and *for* faith—may reflect a variety of *Jewish* views about Jesus during his ministry. Some apparently alleged that Jesus could not be the Messiah since Elijah, the herald of the Messiah, had not yet appeared. (Mark 9:11) Others evidently argued that the Messiah was not expected to come from Galilee, the home district of Jesus. (John 7:52) Others doubted that Jesus was a descendent of King David, a standard requirement for the Messiah. (John 7:40–42; Mark 12:35–37) After the death of Jesus, other issues were raised. Since Jesus had been crucified, he could not have been the Messiah because that great figure was supposed to triumph over his enemies, such as Rome. Gospel responses to that issue are found in Mark 10:33–34, where Jesus expects his execution, and in Matthew 26:54, where his death was seen as necessary to fulfill scripture. Doubts expressed about his resurrection are countered in Mark 16:1–8 and in Matthew 27:62–66. The doubts about Jesus reflected in these Gospel accounts become central in Jewish views about Jesus.

> Much of classical Jewish theological teaching considered Jesus . . . as an apostate who subverted the teachings of Judaism, a Jew whose teachings were utilized by his followers as a justification for the persecution of the Jewish people in many lands over many centuries, and as the paradigmatic false Messiah.[6]

JESUS IN THE TALMUD

The earliest specific Jewish comments about Jesus come from the Babylonian Talmud, fixed in the seventh century CE.[7] In this literature, various rabbis were intent on understanding the Torah ("instruction/learning") and contemplating the correct application of the Torah to daily life. This task was expansive and detailed. For instance, the Ten Commandments given to Moses ruled that the Sabbath should be kept holy and that work should not be done on that day. But that source does not explain what constitutes "work," hence the need to clarify the intent of that law. Is it permissible to walk on the Sabbath? If so, for what reason and for how far? Is it permissible for a farmer to rescue an animal that has fallen into a ditch on the Sabbath? The Talmud examines a great variety of such issues since a clear moral and ritual path for the faithful was crucial. Obedience to the divine law was the means of being in right relationship to the Creator.

The Babylonian Talmud actually says very little about Jesus, but what is stated tends to be denigrating. This attitude toward Jesus is best understood by reflecting on the historical situation. Ancient Roman religion was openly polytheistic, and some of the emperors claimed to be gods and, as such, were due to be worshipped. The basic monotheism of both Judaism and Christianity totally rejected polytheism as well as the presumption of such emperors. Given the power of Rome, this put these monotheistic faiths at high risk. No doubt the Romans were perplexed by the "stubbornness" of such monotheists, since one god more or less seemed not to be a great issue for a polytheist. On the other hand, someone believing in only one god seemed dangerously close to being atheist, especially since no idols or statues were part of the cult.

Various emperors carried out a range of policies that restricted and punished both Jews and Christians. After the destruction of the Jerusalem Temple in 70 CE, Jews and Jewish proselytes were allowed to practice their religion but only if they paid the Jewish tax. Christians suffered persecution in various forms from a range of emperors until Constantine alters the religious scene with the Edict of Milan (313 CE). This Edict ruled that Christianity was to be a tolerated religion. In 380 CE, the Edict of Thessalonica made Nicene Christianity the official religion of the Roman Empire. As Christianity became more linked with the power of the Roman Empire, strictures against Jews and Judaism increased.

History also involved tensions that developed between Judaism and the emerging Christian community. The Christian proclamation of Jesus as the promised Messiah who was to return soon in glory was rejected as without foundation by the rabbis. After the fall of Jerusalem in 70 CE, the Jewish Christian sect in Jerusalem was scattered. At that point, Gentile (non-Jewish) Christianity became the leading voice. This voice carried within it the perspective of Paul, who became known as the apostle to the Gentiles, and is now considered by many historians to be the formative thinker for traditional Christianity. In his letters, Paul writes very little about the teachings *of* Jesus but develops a theology *about* Jesus.[8] This theology maintained that the right relationship with the Creator was now attained through faith in the redeeming work of Christ rather than through obedience to the burden of the Law (Torah).

The Christian story faced by Judaism in those early centuries was that of creedal Christianity, not the teachings of Jesus as such. The Christian message that challenged the rabbis involved a series of related claims: (1) Jesus was born of the Virgin Mary and is the promised Messiah. (2) Jesus is the Divine Son of God and an aspect of the Trinity. (3) In the crucifixion of Jesus, the Divine redeeming act from human sinfulness was accomplished. (4) The right relationship with God is now to be found through faith in the grace of God made active through the work of the Christ—not in obedience to the Torah. (5) Eternal life is promised for those who take part in the New Covenant. (6) This New Covenant was not limited to the Jews but was offered also to the Gentiles, who were welcomed into the community without first becoming Jews. This Christian proclamation, if accepted, would undercut the very foundation of Judaism by rejecting obedience to the Torah as the means of being in right relationship with God. It is small wonder that the rabbis took umbrage at that message and developed a defense against this competing religious message.

Jewish and Christian scholars generally agree that, while the Talmud has some observations about Jesus, these provide no sound historical information about him. The apparent aim of these stories about Jesus is to construct a *counternarrative* to the Christian story as a way of defeating the Christian message and defending Judaism.[9] The rabbinical material does suggest that the writers were quite familiar with some of the Christian Gospels since the counternarratives reflect accounts from those gospels.[10]

This Talmudic material counters the Christian claim that Jesus was born of the Virgin Mary and descended from the line of David by claiming that Jesus was fathered by a Roman soldier, Pandera. Hence, Mary was an adulteress, not a virgin, and Jesus was a bastard who did not have a Jewish father, so he could not be from the Davidic line.

Other accounts in the Talmud insinuate that Jesus, like his mother, was guilty of sexual misconduct by being "unfaithful to his wife and a disgrace to his parents."[11] A connection to the New Testament narrative might be made by suggesting that Jesus had an affair with Mary Magdalene, known as an immoral woman, or that she was the wife of Jesus. This view was also reflected in a recent work of fiction.[12]

The New Testament contains accounts of Jesus healing the sick and casting out demons and of others being healed by calling on the name of Jesus. In response, the rabbis countered that such healing—which they assumed to have taken place—competes with the authority of the rabbis and involves the authority of the heretic Jesus. A story in the Talmud tells of the grandson of a famous rabbi who is saved from choking to death on something he swallowed when a Christian heretic whispered the name of Jesus. In response, the grandfather curses the heretic preferring that his grandson would have died rather than be saved by the name of Jesus.[13]

In contrast to the New Testament accounts of Jesus being crucified by the Romans, the Talmud asserts that Jesus was stoned to death by the Jews in accordance with Jewish law. In this account, Jesus was convicted of sorcery and of leading others into idolatry. Witnesses were given the opportunity of coming to the defense of Jesus, but no one did so. He was then appropriately stoned to death and was also hanged on a tree—a punishment for the most serious of crimes.

A contemporary scholar, Peter Shäfer, maintains, "The most bizarre of all the Jesus stories is the one that tells how Jesus shares his place in the Netherworld with Titus and Balaam."[14] According to these accounts in the Talmud, Titus, the Roman general who led in the destruction of the Jerusalem Temple, is burned over and over again in Hell. Balaam, who sabotaged the Israelites as they attempted to enter the Promised Land, is punished in Hell by being forced to sit in hot semen. Jesus faced a similar fate. He was condemned to sit forever in boiling excrement. "Understood in this way, the story conveys an ironic message: not only did Jesus *not* rise from the dead, he is punished in hell forever; accordingly, his followers—the blossoming Church, which maintains to be the new Israel—are nothing but a bunch of fools, misled by a cunning deceiver."[15]

A JEWISH *HISTORY OF JESUS*

The first Jewish account of Jesus in some detail comes from a tract entitled *Toledot Yeshu* ("The History of Jesus"), which is possibly as old as the sixth century. Little is known about this work in terms of its place of origin or authorship. It reflects Jewish skepticism concerning the Christian message about Jesus. *Toledot Yeshu* tells of how a man of ill repute, Joseph Pandera (a Roman soldier), forced himself upon Miriam (Mary) while posing as Yohanan, an upright man betrothed to Miriam. The child born was named Yehoshua which became Yeshu. As a young student, he showed disrespect to the sages in various ways and also gave his own impudent interpretation of the Law. After some inquiry, it was discovered that he was the illegitimate son of Joseph Pandera, and this made it necessary for Yeshu to flee to Galilee. As an adult, he was able to learn the letters of God's Name from the foundation stone of the Temple. This knowledge gave him the power to perform magic—miracles. Jewish leaders finally arrested him and charged him with sorcery and leading Jews astray. After his execution, his followers reported that his body was missing from the tomb and that he was resurrected. Jewish leaders finally found the explanation when a gardener confessed that he was responsible for burying Yeshu in a garden because he feared that the followers of Yeshu would steal the body and proclaim him as resurrected.[16] This story may be still alive today. According to Michael Cook:

> *Toledot Yeshu* is outrageous, to some disgraceful. While hardly a historical source about the person it describes, it yet accurately reflects the climate of Christian Europe, where Jews, a persecuted minority, were under relentless pressure to convert. A counternarrative impugning Gospel claims of Jesus' virgin birth, miracles, empty tomb, and resurrection was potentially helpful in warding off proselytizers. Unfortunately, this kind of formulation also appears to have markedly shaped and misdirected elements of the popular Jewish mind-set about Jesus for generations to come. Well into the twentieth century, European Jews were still recounting to their offspring Yiddish folkloristic tales about *Yoshke Pandre* (Yeshu [son of] Pandera)![17]

The Talmud and folk-tales such as *Toledot Yeshu* were intended for Jews, especially for those who could read Aramaic and Hebrew. Eventually the denigrating material about Jesus leaked out to the broader Christian community and raised hostility in a variety of quarters. In the thirteenth century, Pope Gregory IX banned the Talmud. "In a letter to the princes of Europe, he asked them to seize all the condemned books on the first Saturday in Lent, 'while the Jews are gathered in the synagogue', and place the haul 'in the custody of our dear sons, the Dominican and Franciscan friars'."[18]

Martin Luther, a Protestant Reformer, wrote a vitriolic anti-Jewish treatise in 1553, *On the Jews and Their Lies*. That work reveals that Luther was aware of the denigrating material against Jesus and Mary in the Talmud and in other Jewish writings.[19] Fear of this kind of blowback from the Christian communities prompted some Jewish leaders to a self-imposed censorship. As late as 1631, Jewish elders in Poland threatened to ban any new edition of material from the Talmud that contained any reference to Jesus.[20]

MOSES MAIMONIDES

No survey of Jewish thought can omit the monumental figure of Moses Maimonides (1135–1204), usually considered the greatest philosopher of Judaism and certainly a towering intellect in his own right. His principal work, *Guide of the Perplexed*, sought to show that there is no necessary conflict between theology, science, and philosophy. The attempt to harmonize faith and reason reflected the reality of another challenging set of ideas—Greek philosophy—that had been discovered and revived by Arabian Muslims. Maimonides adapted the philosophy of Aristotle to show that there need be no conflict between faith and reason in Jewish thought. Throughout his life, Maimonides wrote to defend Judaism against Greek philosophy, Islam, and Christianity. He also had opponents from other Jewish thinkers.[21]

In his limited discussion of Jesus, Maimonides reflects much of the negativity found in the Talmud and the *Toledot Yeshu*. Among the opponents of the Jews, Maimonides lists those who sought to defeat the Jews through argument and evidence, as did some Greeks and Persians. He observes that another attack came from those who combined controversy with conquest. Jesus the Nazarene is cited as a major representative of this group. It is in the context of this discussion where Maimonides notes "may his [Jesus's] bones be ground to dust." In that work, *Epistle to Yemen*, he notes that, although his father was a gentile, Jesus was a Jew since he was born of a Jewish mother. Another remark appears to reflect the view that Jesus was killed by his fellow Jews: "The sages, . . . aware of his aims before his fame became firmly established among the [Jewish] community, treated him as he deserved."[22]

A recent Jewish scholar notes that parts of the Maimonidean Code were published in a bilingual Hebrew/English edition in 1962.

> [The Hebrew text] has been restored to its original purity, and the command to exterminate Jewish infidels appears in it in full: "It is a duty to exterminate them with one's own hands." . . . [T]he Hebrew text goes on to specify the prime examples of infidels who must be exterminated: "Such as Jesus of Nazareth and his pupils, and Tzadoq and Baitos and their pupils, may the name of the wicked rot."[23]

In spite of his opposition to Christianity and Islam, Maimonides did see some role for these religions in the divine plan. He believed that these religions had helped to spread knowledge of God's Law, the Torah, and when they had spread this knowledge to the ends of the earth, the Messiah would appear. In this way the Jewish story shows how both Christianity and Islam have a significant role to play in the final episode of history.[24]

RECONSIDERING JESUS

The shift in Judaism toward a more accommodating and accepting view of Jesus could plausibly be linked to the Protestant Reformation of the sixteenth century. "It is true that, right at the beginning, the Jews welcomed the Reformation, because it divided their enemies."[25] While the Reformation certainly did not reflect a growing acceptance of Judaism, it broke the power of the Catholic Church and undercut any attempt to unify Christians in a single-faith society. The Jews were no longer the only group that did not conform to the Roman Catholic faith. The Reformation, along with Renaissance scholars, also increased interest in the study of the Old Testament, the Hebrew Bible. This, in turn, led ultimately to a major shift in Biblical studies and a reconsideration of Jesus. Jesus—for some Christian as well as Jewish scholars—became emancipated from orthodox Christian doctrine about him and became viewed as a Jewish man of Jewish faith in his own time and place.

Paradoxical as it may seem, the New Testament Gospels—for centuries repudiated by the rabbis—now became a means of freeing Jesus from Christian doctrine and reclaiming him into the Jewish fold. The same Biblical studies also became a means of demonstrating that the Romans were responsible for the crucifixion of Jesus, not the work of his fellow Jews. The old charge against the Jews of being "Christ killers" was undercut. These developments came not so much as a growing "appreciation for Christianity, but as a tool to justify Judaism."[26] Over the decades to come, Biblical studies—by both Christian and Jewish scholars—helped to ameliorate negative feelings that had been present for centuries. The late Jewish Scholar, Samuel Sandmel, reflected this trend: "I know of no area where anti-Jewish feeling, both toward Jews and toward Judaism, is now as rare as it is in the domain of Christian Bible scholars."[27]

EMERGING NEW TESTAMENT SCHOLARSHIP

A German professor of oriental languages, Hermann Reimarus (1694–1768), is often designated as an early figure in modern scholarship about Jesus. In his work, he sought to put Jesus solidly within the context of the Judaism Jesus would have known. Reimarus drew almost exclusively from the gospels of Matthew, Mark, and Luke. In doing this, he anticipated much of recent scholarship that considers John's Gospel to have little of historical worth about Jesus.

The conclusions of Reimarus ran strongly against the traditional Christian story. He denied that Jesus performed miracles. He held that Jesus believed he was the long expected Messiah of Judaism, that he was crucified, and that Jesus' disciples claimed he had been resurrected after they stole his body. Jesus was then transformed by some of his followers into a divine figure and the redeemer of humanity. Since the general public knew little of the world of scholars, his work had little immediate impact.[28] His approach did anticipate much of the skepticism that was to be expressed in the centuries to come.

An interesting transition figure in Jewish scholarship was Isaac Jost (1793–1860), who published a nine-volume work on the history of the Israelites beginning at the time of the Maccabees (second century, BCE). In that work, he recorded some material about Jesus from the Gospels, but he avoided raising questions about the reliability of these accounts. The mere fact that he included some material about Jesus in his work set a pathway for future Jewish scholars to probe such questions in depth.

THE LIFE OF JESUS, BY DAVID FRIEDRICH STRAUSS

In 1835–36, a book was published "that was, and is, a landmark in the history of Gospel scholarship."[29] *The Life of Jesus* was written by David Friedrich Strauss, a German Lutheran professor of philosophy. In pursuing his intent to produce an accurate history, Strauss subjected the miracle accounts to intense analysis. He opposed a rationalizing approach to miracles that was proposed by some in his day. That approach sought to take away the miraculous nature of such events and provided an alternative interpretation. For example, the account of Jesus walking on water would be explained by suggesting that Jesus was really walking on a sandbar that the disciples could not see. Instead of this attempt at rationalization, Strauss preferred to deny the incident altogether. He characterized such Gospel material as "myth."

> Strauss denied as mythical the virgin birth, the genealogies which trace Jesus' ancestry to David, the two accounts of Jesus birth, which Matthew and Luke relate in greatly different ways, and even that Bethlehem was the birthplace, the persecution by Herod of Jesus, the flight of the father of Jesus into Egypt, the visit by Jesus to the Temple, the "transfiguration," the resurrection of Jesus—there is little that he affirms.[30]

Skepticism about the reliability of Gospel accounts reached what would appear to be the ultimate stage in the later work of Bruno Bauer (1809–1882). He followed the path set down by Strauss and agreed that the Gospel writers had invented many of the accounts about Jesus. Bauer moved from that position to a further conclusion—that the Gospel writers had also invented Jesus! Modern New Testament scholars, Christian, Jewish, or otherwise, generally have various levels of doubt about the historical accuracy of the Gospels, but no serious scholar now writes Jesus off as a piece of historical fiction. *That* he existed is generally conceded. *Who* he was, is still a major issue.[31]

ABRAHAM GEIGER ON JESUS AS A JEW

Strauss and Bauer separated many (or all) of the Gospel accounts of Jesus from the grounding of historical fact. Later, liberal Protestant theologians tended to separate Jesus from Christian doctrine by focusing Christian faith on Jesus, himself, instead of belief in dogmas.[32] This move also became part of growing Jewish scholarship. The contribution of Abraham Geiger (1810–1884) was of considerable significance. He was also one of the founders of Reform Judaism. Geiger believed that Jesus is best understood as a member of the Pharisaic movement, which was a liberalizing force within Judaism at that time. "He [Jesus] was a Jew . . . who shared the hopes of his time and who believed that these hopes were fulfilled in him. He did not utter a new thought, nor did he break down the barriers of nationality. . . . He did not abolish any part of Judaism; he was a Pharisee who walked in the way of Hillel."[33]

Geiger's works can be seen as a defense of the Jewish story against the competing stories of Christianity and Islam. Since Jesus was a Jew and remained a Jew, as Geiger posits, Christian doctrine incorporated pagan elements in its development and strayed from the monotheistic core. Geiger argued that Paul brought Jewish monotheism to the pagan world where it became corrupted by doctrines such as the Trinity. He also argued that the most important teachings of Christianity and Islam were derived from Judaism. "Both Christianity and Islam intended nothing more than the spread of Jewish ideas to the pagan world, making them maidservants to the great religious genius of Judaism. . . . both religions were little more than extensions of Judaism."[34] Echoes of Maimonides are found in Geiger.

TENSIONS OVER ZIONISM

Two voices from the early decades of the twentieth century illustrate the tensions that existed in Jewish thought about Jesus during that period: Claude Montefiore (1858–1938), and Joseph Klausner (1847–1958). Tensions between various scholars were related to how the figure of Jesus could be related to Zionism—the developing idea that the Jewish people should return to their homeland and create a Jewish nation. Jewish scholars who resisted Zionism tended to see Judaism as a religion, not as a nation or a people. On the other hand, scholars with a Zionist perspective tended to see Judaism as a people—a nation—committed to their covenant with their God. Each side in this debate had to decide how Jesus might—or might not—fit into their perspective on Zionism.

CLAUDE MONTEFIORE

Claude Montefiore (1858–1938) "represents, perhaps, the furthest a Jew might travel in a positive evaluation of Jesus."[35] Montefiore, a British liberal Jewish scholar and anti-Zionist—"as were most Reform leaders in the early twentieth century"[36] —maintained that since both the Old and the New Testaments had immense impact on European history, any educated Jew should have read the Gospels just as much as the writings of Shakespeare or Milton. While identifying himself as solidly within Judaism, Montefiore expressed considerable admiration for Jesus as a figure reflecting the prophetic voices of the Old Testament. "He [Jesus] announces doom to the unrepentant and the wicked: he comforts the repentant and the seekers; the afflicted and the poor; the humble and the yearning. . . . Jesus was teacher, pastor, and prophet in one, and in this combination too lies something of his originality."[37]

As a man and a scholar, Montefiore wrote with great style and as close to objectivity as might be possible given the subject matter and the historical background of suspicion and persecution. But this attempt at objectivity had its perils. His "disinclination to offend Christianity offended some fellow Jews . . . for there have been Jews . . . who regard any criticism of Christianity which is not strident as the equivalent of capitulation."[38] Appreciation of Jesus might lead to a slippery slope that would end up as conversion. This anxiety is grounded in the long history of persecution by the hands of some of the followers of Jesus. Even today, the "J" word can revive a cluster of emotions. In an essay, Allen Secher tells of a Jewish mother who fears that the name of Jesus would be used in the wedding of her daughter to a Catholic man. She knew "that if she and her parents hear the word 'Jesus' they will be both mortified and embarrassed."[39]

JOSEPH KLAUSNER

In contrast to Montefiore, Joseph Klausner, a Zionist, took a more critical stance toward Jesus while granting that Jesus was a great teacher of morality. "If ever the day should come and [his] ethical code be stripped of its wrappings of miracles and mysticism, the Book of the Ethics of Jesus will be one of the choicest treasures in the literature of Israel for all time."[40]

Klausner grants that Jesus may have had outstanding qualities but also had elements in his teaching that were a danger to Judaism itself by failing to underline the importance of the Jewish people as a nation. Klausner's Zionist view is reflected in his criticism of Jesus.

> Judaism is a national life, a life which the national religion and human ethical principles (the ultimate object of every religion) embrace without engulfing. Jesus came and thrust aside all the requirements of the national life; it was not that he set them apart and relegated them to their separate sphere in the life of the nation: he ignored them completely; in their stead he set up nothing but an ethico-religious system bound up with his conception of the Godhead.[41]

RECENT AND CONTEMPORARY VOICES

Two Jewish voices—recent and contemporary—deserve to be heard: Samuel Sandmel (1911–1979) and Jacob Neusner (born 1932). In his clear and scholarly work, *We Jews and Jesus*, Sandmel gives his own estimation of Jesus: "I can agree that he was a great and good man, but not that he exceeded other great and good men in the excellency of human virtues."[42]

Neusner's perspective focuses on what may well be the crucial issue: Did Jesus deviate from the truths of Judaism in his teachings? Neusner clearly indicates his respect for the teachings of Jesus, but he states his position clearly:

> Jews believe in the Torah of Moses and form on earth and in their own flesh God's kingdom of priests and the holy people. And that belief requires faithful Jews to enter a dissent at the teachings of Jesus, on the grounds that those teachings at important points contradict the Torah. Where Jesus diverges from the revelation by God to Moses at Mount Sinai, he is wrong, and Moses is right.[43]

In another essay, Neusner writes: "Judaism does not reflect on the meaning of Jesus, who enjoys no standing whatsoever in the theology of Judaism and its law." He concludes that essay by observing "at critical points in his teaching, Jesus abandoned the Torah."[44] Neusner's thoughtful reflections provide a clear example of just how one religious story can seek to defend itself against a competing story—*revealed truth* always trumps.

REJECTION OF CHRISTIAN DOCTRINES ABOUT JESUS

Having explored a variety of ways in which Jewish thinkers have come to terms with the figure of Jesus of Nazareth, a summary of why these thinkers reject some traditional Christian doctrines about him is appropriate.

Judaism rejects the central Christian doctrine that Jesus is the longed for Messiah of Israel. The main argument is that Jesus cannot be accepted as the Messiah because he failed to fulfill the messianic expectations: the Jews were not restored to Zion, the Temple was not rebuilt, and he did not bring about a cataclysmic change in human history and the onset of the Kingdom of God.

Judaism repudiates the Trinitarian doctrine which identifies Jesus with the Godhead. For Judaism, this flirts with polytheism and also presumes to elevate a mere man to the level of the divine. Judaism also rejects the doctrine of the virgin birth and denies the claim that Jesus was resurrected from the dead. Crucified by the Romans, he remained dead.

ON GETTING RIGHT WITH GOD: JUDAISM AND CHRISTIANITY

Another major issue that divides Judaism from Christianity is that of how the individual attains right relationship to the Creator. In each faith there is a correlation between the tradition's view of the human *dilemma* and the religious *answer* to that dilemma. Because Christianity and Judaism disagree on the nature of the problem—the human condition—they also disagree on the answer to the problem.

Judaism describes the human problem in terms of disobedience to the Divine Law. This disobedience is not essentially a matter of ignorance; it is more a matter of a corrupt heart that leads the individual astray. Such disobedience results in alienation from God and in God's judgment in a variety of ways. The Hebrew Bible (Old Testament) reflects some elements of collective responsibility wherein the transgression of one person brings calamity on others. But the major focus in Judaism is on the responsibility of the free individual before God. Each person has the capacity to live in obedience to the Divine Law. Failure is a personal failure, not some fault of another. But if one fails, a truly repentant heart before God brings about reconciliation and strength for the days ahead.

In Judaism, then, the answer to the human condition is the gift of the Torah, the Divine Law. While there are wide variations in the way the Torah is interpreted in various Jewish groups, the Torah remains central in each. The Book of the Prophet Micah encapsulates that view in a few lines: "He has told you, O mortal, what is good; and what does the Lord require of you but to do justice, and to love kindness, and to walk humbly with your God?" (Mic. 6:8)

While the Law guides and prescribes the life of the individual Jew, the Law has also shaped and directed the life of the community through something equivalent to civil law. This reflects the strong sense of being a *people* before God. Throughout history, when the Jews had sufficient independence, their communities were essentially governed by the application of the Torah through courts and other procedures. In present day Israel, the influence of Orthodox Judaism is reflected in many of Israel's laws. Even during periods of the Roman Empire and the Middle Ages, Jewish communities were often given the right to a limited form of self-government within their communities.

In contrast, the Christian story holds a more pessimistic view of the human condition. The doctrine of Original Sin—rejected by Judaism—sets forth the view that all human beings stand guilty before God. While linked to the story of Adam and Eve in the Garden of Eden, the doctrine implies the necessity of a gracious act of God in that no mortal has the means of clearing himself or herself from that basic guilt.

The Christian story also holds that God has given the law through the scriptures, but in Christianity the Law has no *saving* function; the law does not serve as means of achieving a right relationship with God. Instead, the Law has other functions in Christian thought. One is the *civil function* wherein the Law is used to govern societies by way of civil laws and related punishments. Another is the *theological function* or the *proper function* of the Law. In this mode, the law functions to show the individual the depth of his or her sin and helps the believer to recognize the absolute need for God's forgiving love. The law, then, is therapeutic—not punitive. It disturbs in order to bring relief. It prepares the person to turn and receive the forgiving and accepting love of God. The prodigal son comes home and is embraced by his father. In this way the law also guards against self-deception and self-righteousness.

For many Christians, God's law also functions as a guide for the Christian life. It clarifies the moral pathway to be pursued as a thankful and loyal response of one who is forgiven, freed, and strengthened. Good works follow as a *response* to the divine love. As the author of the First Epistle of John wrote, "We love *because* he first loved us." (I John 4:19. Author's emphasis)

The contrasts just expressed between Judaism and Christianity are made in terms of *doctrinal* Christianity. It is a contrast between traditional Judaism and the Christ of faith. The same contrast could not be made in terms of the historical Jesus. This underlines a basic theme of this chapter: the major distinctions between Judaism and Christianity are not based on the teachings of Jesus of Nazareth as far as these can be discerned from the Gospels of Matthew, Mark, and Luke. Modern Biblical scholarship has generally separated the teachings of the historical Jesus from the later doctrines declaring the Christ of faith. Contemporary Judaism, then, does not see Jesus, himself, as a figure in opposition to traditional Judaism. Many Jewish scholars now see Jesus as a Jewish man deeply committed to his own understanding of Judaism. Jesus of Nazareth may have strayed from an accurate interpretation of the Torah, as Jacob Neusner suggests, but he can be safely enfolded into Jewish history as a committed Jew rather than an enemy of the faith.

In short, many contemporary Jews conclude that Jesus was not a "Christian." This conclusion would also follow from the definition of "Christian" proposed in Chapter 2: a person who holds Jesus as the central factor of his or her religious faith and life. The conclusion also reflects the observation that Christianity is a religion *about* Jesus, not the religion *of* Jesus.

NOTES

1. See John Gager, *The Origins of Anti-Semitism: Attitudes Toward Judaism in Pagan and Christian Antiquity* (London: Oxford University Press, 1983), and Walter Laqueur, *The Changing Face of Anti-Semitism: From Ancient Times to Present Day* (New York: Oxford University Press, 2006).

2. For a helpful tracing of this history, see Jacob Neusner, "Judaism," in Arvind Sharma, *Our Religions* (San Francisco: HarperCollins, 1993).

3. Neusner in Sharma, 310.

4. David Rhoads, *Israel in Revolution 6–74 CE* (Philadelphia: Fortress Press, 1979).

5. See Paul Johnson, *A History of the Jews* (New York: Harper and Row, 1988) part II for a detailed account of this history.

6. Byron Sherwin, "Who Do You Say That I Am?" in Beatrice Bruteau, *Jesus Through Jewish Eyes* (Maryknoll, N.Y.: Orbis Books, 2001), 31.

7. The Talmud is the basis for Jewish law. It is over 6,200 pages long and contains the teachings and opinions of many rabbis. The subject matter includes law, ethics, philosophy, history, and lore.

8. For a work on Paul by a Jewish scholar, see Samuel Sandmel, *The Genius of Paul* (Minneapolis MN: Fortress Press, 1979).

9. See Peter Schäfer, *Jesus in the Talmud* (Princeton: Princeton University Press, 2007) for a scholarly work that views these Talmudic stories about Jesus as a *counternarrative*. In contrast to earlier Jewish scholars who argued that these accounts were not about Jesus of Nazareth but of some other historical figure, Schäfer maintains that these stories were intended to be about Jesus. Many authors tend to avoid this sensitive material. Harry Freedman, for example, in his *The Talmud: A Biography*, page 116, tends to dismiss the material even though he includes Schäfer's work in his bibliography. A section in a recent scholarly work tends to mute the issue by referring to "alleged" material in the Talmud that contained disparaging comments about Jesus and Mary. The essay notes that the charges led to the burning of Talmudic texts in 1242 as well as prohibition and censoring of the Talmud. The article does not comment on the accuracy of the "allegations" nor does it give any details about the nature of the disparaging comments. Schäfer's book is not listed as a reference in this article. See Judith Baskin and Kenneth Seeskin, editors, *The Cambridge Guide to Jewish History, Religion, and Culture* (New York: Cambridge University Press, 2010), 121.

10. Schäfer for a detailed account of this material.

11. Ibid., 28.

12. Dan Brown, *The Da Vinci Code* (New York: Doubleday, 2005).

13. Schäfer, 11.

14. Ibid., 13.

15. Ibid., 13.

16. For a widely known version of this story, see Morris Goldstein, *Jesus in the Jewish Tradition* (New York: The Macmillan Co., 1950), 148 f.

17. Michael Cook, "Evolving Jewish Views of Jesus," in Bruteau, 18.

18. Johnson, 217.

19. For a survey of the history of anti-Judaism and anti-Semitism during these centuries in Europe, see Johnson, 238 f.

20. Goldstein, 4.

21. For a study of Maimonides, see Joel Kraemer, *Maimonides* (New York: Doubleday, 2008).

22. Kraemer, 238. Here Kraemer explores Maimonides' *Epistle to Yemen*.

23. Israel Shahak, *Jewish History Jewish Religion: the Weight of Three Thousand Years* (London: Pluto Press, 1994) 29–30. Shahak notes that Tzadoq and Baitos were supposed founders of the Sadducee sect.

24. Kraemer, 240.

25. Johnson, 241.

26. Susannah Heschel, "Jewish Views of Jesus," in Gregory Barker, editor, *Jesus in the World Faiths* (Maryknoll, New York: Orbis Books, 2005), 151.

27. Samuel Sandmel, *We Jews and Jesus* (New York: Oxford University Press, 1965), 101.

28. For a substantial overview of this growing scholarship, see Sandmel, Chapter 4.

29. Sandmel, 56.

30. Ibid., 55.

31. See Mark Powell, *Jesus as a Figure in History: How Modern Historians View the Man from Galilee* (Louisville, Kentucky: Westminster John Knox Press, 1998) for a range of views by historians.

32. Some figures would include F. D. E. Schleiermacher (1768–1834), and Adolph Harnack (1851–1934).

33. Heschel, 153.

34. Ibid., 154–155.

35. Barker and Gregg, 46.

36. Sandmel, 91.

37. Barker and Gregg, 52.

38. Sandmel, 89.
39. Allen Secher, "The 'J' Word," in Bruteau, 109.
40. Sandmel, 92. Quoting from Klausner's *Jesus of Nazareth*.
41. Barker and Gregg, 56–57.
42. Sandmel, 110.
43. Jacob Neusner, *A Rabbi Talks with Jesus* (New York: Doubleday, 1993), xii.
44. Jacob Neusner, "Why Jesus has no Meaning to Judaism," in Barker, 173.

Chapter Four

Jesus in Islam

One of the great socio-cultural movements in history took place in the seventh century CE when the religion of Islam emerged. This new faith surged onto a scene which was a maze of polytheism, Judaism, Christianity, and Zoroastrianism. The polytheism was expressed in an ancient shrine, the Ka'ba (the Cube) in the city of Mecca. That shrine contained idols or representations of over 300 gods and goddesses recognized throughout Arabia as protectors of various tribes. In an expression of ecumenicity, images of Jesus and his mother Mary were alongside the many pagan deities.[1] Adding to the complex religious scene were theological tensions among Christian groups as well as disputes between various Jews and Christians.

CALLED TO BE A PROPHET

An Arab trader was profoundly disturbed by the religious condition of his tribal people. His name was Muhammad—Arabic for "most praised one." (ca. 570–632 CE) As a trader, Muhammad learned about religious views and contentions from various sources. He concluded that both Judaism and Christianity had prophets who brought God's message to those communities—Moses for Judaism and Jesus for Christianity; however, no prophet had spoken to the Arab peoples. A deeply religious man, Muhammad was troubled not only by the religious confusion and contentions of the time but also by the social conditions among his own peoples. Especially problematic was the great disparity between the wealthy and the poor as well as the plight of women and orphans. In a quest for a possible solution, he would spend time meditating. One night, while meditating, a powerful presence overwhelmed him and commanded him to "recite." This encounter marks the beginning of a new revelation—the Quran—and the birth of a new faith—Islam. As the revelations to Muhammad continued, he came to believe that he had been called to be a prophet. His wife, Khadija, supported him and became the first believer.

As is often the case with those called as prophets, Muhammad became a threat to powerful interests in his home city of Mecca. His life threatened, he escaped to Yathrib (later called Medina) in 622 CE with a number of his followers. This becomes year 1 in the Islamic calendar, the beginning of Islam as a community of faith ruled by that faith. It also became the time when Muhammad took on the role of statesman. In Yathrib, he united the various communities—Arab, Christian, and Jewish—by formulating the Constitution of Medina. After a number of unsuccessful attacks on him and his community by enemies from Mecca, those early enemies relented and became part of the faith. Muhammad moved back to Mecca victoriously and declared a general amnesty for his former enemies. This act of compassion and tolerance was to leave an impact on the future of Islam.

THE SPREAD OF ISLAM

The new religion gathered strength and numbers as various Arab tribes converted. By the end of his life in 632 CE, Muhammad had brought most of the Arab tribes into the new community of faith, although not all joined with great enthusiasm. After Muhammad died, the faith was led by a series of his followers, and the spread of Islam beyond Arabia was extensive and swift. Within a century of the beginning of the faith, Muslim armies moved across North Africa into Spain and were finally halted at the Battle of Tours, France, in 732. They also had reached east as far as the Indus Valley in the eighth century. By the twenty-first century, Islam had become the second largest religion in the world, after Christianity, and now numbers some 1.6 billion followers. While Islam originated in Arabia, only about twenty percent of the world's Muslims are from Arab countries. Large Muslim communities are currently found in India, Indonesia, Pakistan, and Bangladesh. By any standard, these results mark Muhammad as one of the Great Men of history.

ISLAM ROOTED IN THE PROPHETIC TRADITIONS OF JUDAISM AND CHRISTIANITY

Islam comes onto the scene centuries after the origins of Judaism and Christianity. Consequently, the new religion had to come to terms with both of these established faiths. The Quran contains considerable material about both of these earlier monotheisms and also provides a means for Muslims to relate to these faiths. Islam accepts that there are earlier revelations, such as the

Hebrew Bible (Old Testament) and the New Testament, but, according to Islam, there are confusions and inaccuracies in both of those traditions that need to be clarified through the new revelation—the Quran. Islam, then, becomes "the straight path."[2]

Muslims believe that the Quran was revealed to Muhammad over a period of some twenty-three years. These revelations began when he was forty years of age and continued until the year of his death. While the Quran came through Muhammad, traditional Muslims believe that he was neither the editor nor the author of the work. Instead, the Quran is considered to be the literal word of God, eternal in nature, and preserved in the Arabic language.

JESUS IN THE QURAN

Any attempt to trace the teachings of the Quran about Jesus must be expressed with some caution and modesty. Originally in Arabic, the Quran is a complex work that deserves considerable study and reflection. Muslims consider that the true Quran must be in Arabic; therefore, any translation into another language is *not* the Quran. Several scholars honor that view when translating the Quran into English.[3] The task of translating is a challenge since some passages in the Quran appear to be ambiguous; furthermore, the meaning of the various passages must be understood within the context of Muhammad's lifetime.

NAMES AND TITLES FOR JESUS IN THE QURAN

Jesus is mentioned some thirty-five times in the Quran. The name *Isa* (Jesus) is used many times. He is also given the title of Messiah (Christ) and Son of Mary. Other names include Messenger, Prophet, Spirit and Word. These terms need to be understood in the context of the passage cited and in the light of the meaning given to those terms in the Quran itself.

WHAT THE QURAN DENIES ABOUT JESUS

Before exploring what the Quran says about Jesus, it is helpful to first note what the Quran *denies* or does not say about Jesus. Given the absolute emphasis on the oneness of God—strict monotheism—the Quran rejects the Christian claim that Jesus is divine and the Son of God. The Christian doctrine of the Trinity suggests a polytheism Islam rejects. The claim that God had a son is viewed in the Quran as most absurd: "So believe in God and His Messengers, and say not, 'Three.' Refrain: better is it for you. God is only One God. Glory be to Him—and that He should have a son!" (4:168 f.) According to the Quran, Jesus is a great man, a prophet, but he is only a man.

While the Christian tradition underlines the death by crucifixion and the resurrection of Jesus, the Quran rejects both claims. A passage, with a variety of possible translations, has the Jews saying, "'We slew the Messiah, Jesus son of Mary, the Messenger of God'—yet they did not slay him, neither crucified him, only a likeness of that was shown to them . . . and they slew him not of a certainty—no indeed." (4:155 f.) The claim that the Jews killed Jesus does have a Jewish source since it appears in the Talmud.

This passage from the Quran may mean that the Jews *believed* they killed Jesus, but did not actually *kill* him. Or the passage may mean that they thought they killed *Jesus* but they killed *someone else* instead. The latter belief was held at that time by some Gnostic Christian sects who argued that, if Jesus were truly divine, he could not have been killed. In other passages, the Quran insists that Messengers of God can be killed only by an act of God, whose will is the foundation of all events. Jesus, being one of the Messengers (along with Moses and Muhammad), could not have been defeated by mere mortals.

MARY AS VIRGIN MOTHER OF JESUS

While the Quran rejects the Christian account of the death of Jesus, it parallels in many ways the New Testament view of Mary, the mother of Jesus. No other woman is mentioned by name in the Quran, but Mary is mentioned more often in the Quran than she is in the New Testament and is considered to be a perfect example of a woman of faith. In the Quran, Mary is seen as someone perfectly submitted to God's will, which is illustrated in her conception of Jesus. The Quran accepts the Christian doctrine of the Virgin Birth and defends Mary against accusations of unchastity. According to the Quran, the infant Jesus defends his mother's innocence (19:27–34). No human father was involved in the conception. Joseph, Mary's husband according to the Christian tradition, is not mentioned in the Quran.

The virgin birth of Jesus is the result of the direct will of an omnipotent God.

> "Lord," said Mary, "how shall I have a son seeing no mortal has touched me?"
> "Even so," God said, "God creates what He will. When He decrees a thing He does but say to it 'Be,' and it is." (3:40 f.)

According to the Quran, even though Jesus was born of a virgin, he is *not* to be construed as divine or as the Son of God.

JESUS AS *MESSIAH*

Throughout the Quran, Jesus is given the title (or name) of Messiah eleven times. The title is used in the Quran as way of speaking of Jesus as a messenger of God and as a prophet in the tradition of the Old Testament. The title "Messiah" in the Quran does not carry the meaning as in Judaism, where the Messiah is seen as the One to come and bring God's kingdom into the world; neither does the title carry the meaning of the Messiah (Christ, the anointed one) of the Christian scriptures as savior and redeemer.

JESUS AS A PROPHET

In the Quran, Jesus is spoken of as a prophet and messenger along with many of the other prophets of the Old Testament. The task of the prophet is to bring guidance to a community from God. Among the prophets noted in the Quran, Moses is a prophet who brought the Tawrah (Torah) to the Jewish people; likewise, Jesus is a prophet who brought the Injil (Gospel) as guidance to the Christian community. According to the Quran, while Jesus is an important figure in this prophetic tradition, Muhammad has a special place as the final and comprehensive prophet. This final revelation was needed, according to the Muslims, because both the Jewish and the Christian communities had allowed errors to enter into their religious beliefs and practices. For the Muslims, prophecy ended with the role of Muhammad. He is considered the last of the prophets—the Seal. In Islam, Muhammad is never considered to be divine.

JESUS AS SPIRIT OR WORD

The Quran also speaks of Jesus as *Spirit* or *Word*:

> People of the Book, go not beyond the bounds in your religion, and say not as to God but the truth. The Messiah, Jesus son of Mary, was only the Messenger of God, and His Word that He committed to Mary, and a Spirit from Him. So believe in God and His Messengers, and say not, "Three." (4:168 f.)

One commentator suggests that Jesus is called "a word" because he came into existence directly by a spoken word by God, not by way of a human father. The word "Spirit" is used in reference to Jesus seven times in the Quran, though the meaning appears to be obscure. Most commentators appear to agree that Jesus is called "*a* Spirit," not "*the* Spirit." According to the Quran, the Spirit was active in the birth of Jesus and is also described as a support for Jesus as a child, youth, and man. Similar references to Jesus and the Spirit are found in the New Testament Gospels at the time of Jesus's baptism and when he performed miracles. (Mk. 1:10; Lk. 4:14)

JESUS AS A MIRACLE WORKER

Jesus is also described in the Quran as a worker of miracles:

> When God said, "Jesus Son of Mary, remember My blessing upon thee and upon thy mother, when I confirmed thee with the Holy Spirit, to speak to men in the cradle, and of age; and when I taught thee the Book, the Wisdom, the Torah, the Gospel; and when thou createst out of clay, by My leave, as the likeness of a bird, and thou breathest into it, and it is a bird, by My leave; and thou healest the blind and the leper by My leave, and thou bringest the dead forth by My leave." (5:108 f.)

The miracle of making clay birds that fly away is not in New Testament documents but is cited in the *Infancy Gospel of Thomas*. The story also appears in the Jewish *Toledot Yeshu* (Life of Jesus) and other non-canonical works from various Christian sources. The Quran indicates that the miracles of Jesus were looked upon by the Jews as some kind of sorcery. The Talmud also has passages to that effect. In the Quran, the miracles of Jesus are seen as a way that God's power confirms the message of Jesus, but those miracles are always seen as acts of *God's* power, not of Jesus's alone. It is of some interest that the Quran never asserts that Muhammad performed miracles although later Muslim traditions make this claim. Muhammad did view the Quran—as revealed through the power of God—as a miracle.

WORDS FROM JESUS IN THE QURAN

While the Quran has many verses relating to the teachings of Jesus that have some parallels in the Gospels, it does not repeat any words of Jesus directly. On the other hand, the Quran has a number of verses cited as the words of Jesus. One such passage links Jesus's sayings to the coming of Muhammad: "And when Jesus son of Mary said, 'Children of Israel, I am indeed the Messenger of God to you, confirming the Torah that is before me, and giving good tidings of a Messenger who shall come after me, whose name shall be Ahmad.'" (61:6) Variants on that verse do not mention Ahmad, but the quotation above is the official one, and Muslim scholars widely agree that the Messenger prophesied by Jesus is Muhammad.

THE MISSION OF JESUS AS EXPRESSED IN THE QURAN

One passage in the Quran outlines the mission of Jesus and repeats some material stated in other passages in the Quran:

> And He [God] will teach him [Jesus] the Book, the Wisdom, the Torah, the Gospel, to be a Messenger to the Children of Israel saying, "I have come to you with a sign from your Lord. I will create for you out of clay as the likeness of a bird; then I will breathe into it, and it will be a bird, by the leave of God, I will also heal the blind and the leper, and bring to life the dead by the leave of God. I will inform you too of what things you eat, and what you treasure up in your houses. Surely in that is a sign for you if you are believers. Likewise confirming the truth of the Torah that is before me, and to make lawful to you certain things that before were forbidden unto you. I have come to you with a sign from your Lord; so fear you God, and obey you me. Surely God is my Lord and your Lord; so serve Him. This is a straight path." (3:43–44)

The Quran does not view Jesus as one who brings a *new* message to the people of Israel; rather, he is another—and final—messenger to the Jews. Jesus confirms the revelations that had been given to the Jews (Torah) and corrects distortions that had developed within the Jewish tradition. The revelations that come through Muhammad—the Quran—are given to the Arab peoples, but these revelations also stand as the consummation of the prophetic voices in the history of Israel and Christianity.

THE DEATH OF JESUS

Included in the Quran are passages about the death of Jesus, but the meanings of those passages have been debated by Muslim scholars. The Quran clearly maintains that Jesus was not killed by the Jews, nor was he crucified. However, the Quran does not clearly indicate what finally happened to Jesus. A number of passages refer to the death of Jesus, but the following is one of the most important:

> So, for their [Jews] breaking the compact, and disbelieving in the signs of God, and slaying the Prophets without right, and for their saying, "Our hearts are uncircumcised"—nay, but God sealed them for their unbelief, so that they believe not, except a few—and for their unbelief, and their uttering against Mary a mighty calumny, and for their saying, "We slew the Messiah, Jesus son of Mary, the Messenger of God"—yet they did not slay him, neither crucified him, only a likeness of that was shown to them. Those who are at variance concerning him surely are in doubt regarding him; they have no knowledge of him, except the following of surmise; and they slew him not of a certainty—no indeed; God raised him up to Him; God is All-mighty, All-wise. (4:154 f.)

What, then, really did happen to Jesus? Did he ever die? A variety of interpretations have been offered. A traditional view within Islam is that the Jews did try to kill Jesus but were unable to kill him. This leaves a variety of possible explanations. One account states that Jesus went into hiding, and one of his companions was killed instead. Another account holds that a great cloud of darkness was sent by God along with angels to protect Jesus. This led to Judas being crucified in his place.

SOMEONE ELSE WAS CRUCIFIED INSTEAD OF JESUS

A number of Muslim writers adopted the idea that some other person was substituted for Jesus at the crucifixion. Possible substitutes included Simon of Cyrene, Judas, Pontius Pilate, and an enemy of Jesus. On the other hand, some modern Muslim scholars reject this *substitute* victim story as unworthy of consideration. It should be noted that no passage in the Quran makes the claim that someone else was crucified in place of Jesus.

Accounts of someone killed as a substitute for Jesus occur in a number of sources which date back to the second century CE, long before the life of Muhammad. Some Gnostic Christians held that Jesus was a divine intelligence that only *appeared* to be in human form. When the enemies of Jesus attempted to crucify him, he changed his form and Simon of Cyrene was crucified in his place. The Gnostic argument seemed to be that, if Jesus was truly divine, then he could not be killed. In the Gospel accounts of Jesus's death, Simon of Cyrene was the one who carried the cross for Jesus after he stumbled under the load. According to these Gnostics, Jesus stood by, watched the error, and then ascended into heaven.

WHAT FINALLY HAPPENED TO JESUS?

If Jesus was not crucified, then what finally happened to him according to the Quran? Since the accounts in the Quran provide no definitive answer to the question of the death of Jesus, a number of views have been expressed by Muslims. Any interpretation must come to terms with passages from the Quran that allude to the death of Jesus. One has Jesus saying "Peace be upon me, the day I was born, and the day I die, and the day I am raised up alive." (19:34) A common view in Islam is that God took Jesus to Himself just as God had taken up the prophet Elijah. This, however, still leaves open the question of his death.

Another view suggests that Jesus actually remained on the cross for a few hours but did not die there. He was taken down by his disciples and hidden from his enemies. An Ahmadiyya Muslim belief extends this view by claiming that Jesus finally ventured into Kashmir and died there. Another account posits that Jesus died on the cross, but it was the death of his body only. A passage from the Quran reflects this possible view: "Count not those who are slain in God's way as dead, but rather living with their Lord." (3:163) A consistent emphasis in all these perspectives is that the Jews rejected Jesus, God's Messenger, and they intended to kill him.

CONTRASTING VIEWS OF JESUS: ISLAM AND CHRISTIANITY

Accounts of the crucifixion and resurrection of Jesus do point to a significant difference between the traditional Christian view of Jesus and that of Islam. In the Christian account, the crucifixion and resurrection of Jesus are central to the atoning sacrifice of Jesus for the fallen race of humanity. Since Islam rejects the Christian doctrine of original sin from which every human being must be redeemed, it has no need for a divine redeemer. Islam has a prophet, but no "savior" figure. Instead, much like Judaism, Islam holds that God has shown the way and that persons are responsible for their own salvation. Islam also emphasizes that God is compassionate and forgiving.

JESUS AND THE END TIMES

Like Orthodox Judaism and traditional Christianity, Islam also has an understanding of the "end times" or eschatology. Zoroastrian views about the end times are the oldest known and are carried over in some forms into Judaism and Christianity. In Zoroastrianism, the end times are seen as the final victory of the good God over the forces of evil, the establishment of some ideal state of affairs, the punishment of the wicked and the reward of the faithful and good. The message of the coming of this time of tribulation echoes throughout Western history and can be heard clearly in our own times.

The earliest surahs (chapters) in the Quran often include vivid descriptions of the coming of God's judgment and the end times. In Islam, Jesus becomes a figure in this coming history. A passage in the Quran about Jesus states, "There is not one of the People of the Book but will assuredly believe in him before his death, and *on the Resurrection Day he will be a witness against them.*" (4:157 f. Emphasis added) The Hadith—a collection of words and deeds of Muhammad and second only to the Quran in its authority—expresses the belief that Jesus awaits in Heaven until the end times. He will then descend to the earth and lead a battle against the anti-Christ. At that time, Jesus will also assert that Muhammad is the final Messenger of God.

Chapter 4

DIVISIONS WITHIN ISLAM

By their basic nature, religions generate a variety of splinter groups and sects. The division between Sunni and Shi-ite Islam occurred within fifty years of Muhammad's death, when a disagreement arose about leadership of the community of believers after the death of Muhammad. Tensions between these groups still exist. Other splinter groups developed later and were deemed heretical by many traditional Muslims. The Ahmadiyas and the Sufis are two such groups.

AHMADIYA MUSLIMS

An Indian Muslim, Mirza Ghulam Ahmad (ca.1836–1908), linked a number of themes from within Islam to create the movement that bears his name. He had been disturbed by Muslims who showed antipathy and violence toward Christians and who also claimed that Jesus would return to bring such nonbelievers to judgment. Ahmad recognized that most Muslims and Christians believed that Jesus ascended alive to Heaven and is awaiting his return to earth. Their stories about the nature of his return varied. Ahmad added to this account by asserting that Jesus had actually spent some time in India after he had recovered from the attempt to crucify him. Jesus had gone to India as part of his mission to seek the lost sheep of Israel—some of whom were in India.

Ahmad was also aware of a belief held by some Muslims that a *Mahdi* (a divinely inspired leader, now hidden) would arrive to lead Muslims. Ahmad claimed to be that long awaited figure. Drawing from the Bible, he became convinced that he was also the Messiah—Jesus in his second coming. Adding to that, he claimed to be a reappearance of Muhammad. Although making these broad claims, Ahmad did not claim to be a *new* prophet. He evidently thought of himself as a mouthpiece for Muhammad and that his mission was to bring a message of humility and peace back into Islam. For most traditional Muslims, Ahmad's claim to be the Mahdi placed him outside the fold of Islam. His view of Jesus was, however, consistent with traditional Islam: Jesus was a prophet of God, but he was not divine, not a son of God, and not crucified.

Ahmad rejected the idea of a bloody messiah in either Christian or Muslim form and insisted that holy war (jihad) was to be carried out only by preaching—without violence. The movement itself splintered into a variety of sects. One sect rejected the more extreme claims made by Ahmad but still considers him to be a man who helped to renew Islam as a religion of peace. Even today, Ahmadiya Muslims are pacifist and are active in missionary work in England, the United States, Africa, and the East Indies.

THE SUFIS: MUSLIM MYSTICISM

For deeply religious persons, there is often a great thirst for experiencing the presence of the divine—an emotional experience that moves beyond creeds and intellectual formulations. This thirst is often linked to an ascetic tendency that moves away from the glitter of power and material gain. For these souls, the things of this world count as little; relationship with God is all. Muslim Mystics—the Sufis—are prime examples of this religious mood. Their *mysticism* involved the quest for such a deep love of God that the individual is *annihilated* by way of union with the divine. This sense of union with God was expressed by a Persian Sufi, al-Hallaj, when he uttered, "I am the True." For his apparent ultimate blasphemy of claiming that he was God, he was cruelly put to death. Later Sufis interpreted his utterance in a way that escaped such blasphemy, but in doing so they walked a dangerous line. Sufis have had their martyrs. While they found a basis for such beliefs in the Quran, this mysticism almost certainly had roots in Greek philosophy—especially developments out of Plato. This mysticism is reflected in the poetry of the Persian Sufi, Jalaluddin Rumi (1207–1273).

In the early centuries of Islam, Sufis represented a protest against the power, pomp, and wealth that had come with the expansion of Islam. They also believed that the rigid formality of much religious practice was superficial and spiritually empty. In their search for a fulfilling faith, they found models in their great prophets. Consistent with traditional Islam, the Sufis considered Muhammad to be the ideal human model who reflected both mercy and justice in his own lifestyle and in his governing of the Muslim community during his lifetime.

While Jesus never governed a community, the Sufis found in him a model for the human venture. By blending the Quran with the life and teachings of Jesus, they pursued an ascetic lifestyle with the practice of humility and poverty. Like ascetics from many faiths, they believed that attachment to things of this world leads persons away from a deep relationship with God—the immediate realization of divine love. Baubles and gadgets are toys for children, but they distract from the truly fulfilling life. Jesus, for the Sufis, demonstrated the ability to avoid compromise with the things of this world and embodied a life of submission to God. In various forms, this asceticism is echoed in Hinduism, Buddhism, Judaism, and Christianity. Saint Francis of Assisi embodied the same view. Reformer Martin Luther observed, "That to which your heart clings is truly your god." American philosopher, William James, reflected this theme in his observation about "the bitch-goddess Success." Sufis agree with Jesus: "For where your treasure is, there shall your heart be also." (Matthew 6:21)

RELIGIONS AS COMPETING COMPLEX MEMES

In the opening chapter, the theory of religions as memes was explored. (Memes are ideas, behavior, or style that spread from person to person.) This theory suggests that memes, like genes, often have other memes competing for space and survival. Religious stories compete with other religious stories. Islam has proven itself to be a successful meme. This faith story or meme can best be summarized in the declaration of faith (shahada) that makes one a Muslim: "There is no God but God and Muhammad is the Messenger of God." This chapter's review of the place of Jesus in Islam explored the tensions between Islam and the other two monotheistic faiths, Judaism and Christianity, which are also memes.

The question for the new faith of Islam was how this new revelation can be affirmed, not only in terms of its continuity with the earlier faiths, but also in terms of basic disagreements. The perspective of Islam seeks to show that God has given differing communities their own law and guidance. In summary form, the faith of Islam makes three claims: (1) God sent the Torah to the Jews to give them guidance. (2) God sent Jesus, who confirms the Torah. (3) Finally, God sent the Quran to the Arabs through Muhammad, and this Quran confirms the earlier revelations and also makes necessary corrections to errors that crept into the earlier faiths.

The third claim—which is a matter of faith and not the conclusion of an argument—is the basic claim of Islam. In this way, the differences between the revelations can be explained and defended by Muslims, resulting in a story (meme) that has been very successful in terms of survival and influence. The figure of Jesus is respectfully folded into the Muslim story by viewing him as a Prophet of God, but in no way divine.

CHRISTIAN ERRORS ABOUT JESUS

The Quran pays great respect to Jesus; nevertheless, it holds that the Christian story in its creedal forms is profoundly mistaken. Both faiths agree that Jesus was a Great Man, but they disagree about the nature of that man. The Quran consistently declares that God is One; hence any claim that Jesus is divine is patently false. For Islam, the doctrine of the Trinity is a form of polytheism to be rejected. These contesting religious stories clashed on this basic disagreement about the prophet from Nazareth.

ON GETTING RIGHT WITH GOD: ISLAM AND CHRISTIANITY

Other theological disputes between Islam and Christianity arise from this fundamental difference between the views of Jesus in the two faiths. The entire story of how human beings come into right relationship with God is at stake. Each faith understands that the situation of human beings is problematic and that human beings are in need of divine assistance. But the *diagnosis* of the nature of that problem and the *prescription* of an answer differ between these faiths.

Islam holds that God has shown the way through the prophets, and it is up to the individual to walk in the way of guidance given—the "straight path." Islam and Judaism largely agree on this point. Both Islam and Judaism hold that each person is responsible and that each person has the capacity to follow God's guidance and to live a life acceptable to God. On the other hand, traditional Christianity asserts that the human situation is more problematic and that only God's grace can finally bring about right relationship between creature and creator. In brief, the Christian story declares a savior; the Muslim story presents a prophet.

According to Islam, one Great Man of history, Jesus of Nazareth, is highly regarded in the revelations received by another Great Man, Muhammad. However, in Islam, Jesus is and remains only a man, neither a Son of God nor a divine being.

NOTES

1. Citations from the Quran in this book are from A. J. Arberry, *The Koran Interpreted* (New York: Simon and Schuster, first Touchstone Edition, 1996). Helpful works about Islam include: Reza Aslan, *No God But God: The Origins, Evolution, and Future of Islam* (New York: Random House, 2005); John Esposito, *Islam: The Straight Path* (New York: Oxford University Press, 2010); and Geoffrey Parrinder, *Jesus in the Quran* (London: Oneworld: Publications, 2013). Parrinder's book provided much of the material for this chapter.

2. Some basic terms: "Islam" is the name of the faith, with the meaning of peace through surrender to God. "Muslim" (Moslem) identifies a follower of the faith. "Allah" is a transliteration of the Arabic term which is translated into English as "God." In Islam, Allah is considered to be the God also worshipped by both Jews and Christians. The name of the holy book of Islam is transliterated from the Arabic variously as Koran, Qu'ran, or Quran., and can be translated as "recitation."

3. For instance, *The Koran Interpreted*, a translation by A. J. Arberry, which is the translation cited in this work. Also *The Meaning of the Glorious Koran*, a translation by Mohammad Marmaduke Pickthall. Neither called their translation *The Koran*, thus honoring the Muslim view.

Chapter Five

Jesus in Hinduism

When Christian missionaries brought their story of Jesus to India, they addressed a culture with stories vastly different from their own. A brief overview of Hinduism to highlight some of these differences will aid in understanding the reactions to Christianity by various Hindu voices. While rites, ceremonies, and patterns of worship are crucial to all religions, this overview of Hinduism will center largely on the beliefs that ground those activities. This brief overview must be selective and will not present a detailed account of this rich and complex tradition.[1]

Differences between Christianity and Hinduism are reflected in the contrasting cosmologies underlying each story. Cosmology is the study of the universe, its origin, and its destiny. Human interest in the origins of all things is pervasive, and myths of origins (cosmogonic myths) abound in all cultures. A seven-year old child once asked, "Where do they get dirt?" The question was as penetrating as its more abstract phrasing: Why is there something rather than nothing? That is a basic question in cosmology.

CHRISTIAN COSMOLOGY

The Christian cosmology, shared with Judaism and Islam, posits that the universe is finite in time. There was a time when the universe did not exist—assuming "time" has any meaning in the absence of a universe. The Genesis creation myths tell of the universe brought into being by the creative act of God. The universe had a beginning and will also have a goal when God's creative act comes to completion. History is serious business; it has a Purpose, an End, and a Fulfillment. "While Hindus and Buddhists sought ways *out of* history, Christianity and Islam sought ways *into* history. Instead of promising escape from experience, these sought meaning in experience." [2]

The Genesis creation story does not directly imply creation *ex nihilo* (out of nothing), but later Christian philosophers and theologians made that assertion.[3] While the creation is a product of God's actions, it is not divine nor is it a development out of the divine life itself. The universe is a created creature, not an emanation from or an aspect of God. God as creator is wholly other. God is God; creation is always less than divine.

Creation as non-divine is also dependent on the sustaining power of God and is finite in the sense that it can cease to be. Since created creatures are finite, death is real and created creatures can die. Human beings, as created creatures, have death as part of their journey. "You are dust, and to dust you shall return." (Genesis 3:19) The Christian hope is that death, the "last enemy," has been defeated. Christian creeds do not speak of an immortal soul as some spark from a divine fire or source. Instead, they posit the "resurrection of the body," a belief shared with Judaism and Islam.[4] This doctrine affirms that only God is essentially immortal while human life beyond the death of the body always depends on the will and power of God. But the resurrected faithful retain an identity of their own, as distinct from God. The resurrected person remains in relation to his or her creator and is not absorbed into the Divine with the loss of personal identity.

CHRISTIAN ANTHROPOLOGY

Related to this cosmology is what can be called Christian anthropology or the Christian understanding of human beings. In brief, the Christian story holds that human beings are created and sustained by the power of God. The original pair, Adam and Eve, was placed in a peaceful garden that contained all that the couple needed. Death was not part of the scene. Even the animals were vegetarians. In disobedience to God, the couple violated God's will and was, as a consequence, cast out of Eden (the Fall) and into a world of toil, suffering, and death. Sin entered into the story. The Christian narrative, then, is the story of God's intention to redeem and bring the human community back into a healed relationship with the Creator. God achieves this redemption in part through the giving of divine law to guide them in their brokenness and ignorance. The final gracious act of God is that of divine redemption through the life, death, and resurrection of Jesus the Christ (Messiah). For the Christian believer, right relationship with God is attained through faith in this redemptive work. This faith is, itself, a gift. Sin is overcome. Death is defeated. The Christian anticipates an eternity in the blissful presence of God with the blessed community of the saved. Eternal *communion* of the person with God is the hope—not *union* or merging with God and the loss of individuality.

HINDU COSMOLOGY

Hindu cosmology differs strikingly. The early formulation of this cosmology comes from the Vedas ("sacred knowledge"), early Hindu scriptures that may date back as far as 1500 BCE. Myths of creation in these works took various forms, but a basic theme prevailed: the universe and all it contains is an expression of divine reality itself. Early stories tell of some original being (man, cow, or horse) who through self sacrifice brought the universe into being. The universe is, then, an expression of and identical with that original divine figure. Another image is that of a Golden egg that blossoms forth into a universe. As the stories get refined, the original source is commonly called *Brahman*, who brings the world into being out of himself. (The masculine gender seems basic in these stories, although Hinduism has prominent places for goddesses.)

These stories of origins raise the question of time. Was there a time when the universe was not? Is the universe eternal? Will there be a time when the universe ceases to be or gets transformed into some ultimate goal? These issues are addressed in a theory of the cyclic nature of reality. The universe does flow out of the divine life, but over vast eons of time, it will collapse back, again, into that One. This collapse is sometimes referred to as the "night of Brahman." In another vast expanse of time, the universe blossoms out or flows forth again from that One. This pattern continues as an eternal recurrence and reflects a cyclic view of history. The process has no "beginning" and has no "end." This story is in sharp contrast to the Christian story of beginning and end—a linear view of history. Distinctions between these two views of history are reflected also in musical traditions in the West and East. In sharp contrast to Italian operas and much of Western music, traditional Hindu music has little sense of beginning, middle, or end.[5]

The Hindu view of humanity grows out of and flows from the cosmology. Human beings are part of the eternal processes of Brahman. Correctly understood, human beings are expressions of this divine activity and are seen in various Hindu scriptures as identical with the divine. The true self of the human being—*atman*—is identical with the essence of the divine—Brahman. "Thou art that." Our usual sense of an individual existence is, in some sense, an illusion (*maya*). Given the identity of atman to Brahman, human beings are, in reality, immortal. They are uncreated and deathless. In one philosophical stroke, the problems of identity (What am I?) and death are overcome. This view is illustrated in the Hindu classic, the *Bhagavad Gita* (Sacred Song). Arjuna, the hero of the story, is about to go into battle against his kinsmen. He finds himself in a dilemma since his duty as a warrior is to fight, yet his basic ethics instruct him not to kill his kinsman. The dilemma is solved when the god figure, Krishna, counsels him. Arjuna need not fear the results of the battle; he has only to do his duty as a warrior. Furthermore, the essence of those he faces in battle is not their perishable body but their eternal soul. No one in the battle can be truly killed. Arjuna must do his warrior caste duty and not be concerned about the outcome of his actions. He must act without desire for reward or fear of punishment.

Central to the Hindu view of the humanity are the concepts of *samsara, dharma, karma,* and *moksha*. These four concepts outline the human dilemma and the proposed solution. Samsara is the cycle of rebirth or reincarnation. Just as the cosmic process is one of eternal cyclic repetition, so the individual soul is caught up in a cycle of death, rebirth, death, and rebirth. For Hinduism, this is *not* good news. The prospects are daunting. The nature of rebirthing, the type of life into which persons are reborn, depends upon the moral quality of the previous life they lived.

The moral guidelines are expressed in dharma, the concept of duty or law built into the nature of existence. Dharma is the moral pathway and leads to significant consequences. The good or evil deeds of a lifespan result in an accumulation of karmic consequences that determine the nature of the next cycle of life. This "law of karma" can be thought of as a moral law of cause and effect. Good karmic accumulation can, for instance, result in being reborn higher in the caste system or social system of the community. Bad karma can lead to being reborn in a life at a lower level of existence, a beast or insect. The caste system of India is a reflection of karmic law in operation. The caste into which a person is born is the result, for good or ill, of the deeds of that person's past life. This view, perhaps, made it possible for the members of any of the castes, high or low, to accept their situation as basically in keeping with the nature of things. Karmic Law says "You get what you deserve."

THE GOAL OF MOKSHA — RELEASE

The ultimate goal or hope of traditional Hinduism is to escape from the oppressive cycles of samsara. This final release is moksha, liberation from bondage to the cycle of death and rebirth. Reflecting the great complexity of Hinduism, this release can be achieved in a variety of ways. The philosophically inclined tend to think of moksha as a merging with the divine reality and the loss of individuality. Moksha is to *experience* "Thou art that." The analogy might be that of a drop of water, once whipped into the air by the winds of life, dropping back into and merging with the great Sea of the Divine. While the drop was in the air, it may have thought of itself as an individual with an independent existence. Yet that drop's sense of independent, individual existence is an illusion (*maya*), even as our human sense of individual existence is an illusion. The drop of water finally realizes that such individuality was an illusion as it blends, again, into the great Sea. That great Sea is Brahman. "Thou art that."

But not all human beings are philosophically inclined; they think of moksha in more individual terms. Some would consider total loss of individuality by way of merging into the Divine to be an empty prospect. These persons think of moksha as a blissful *communion* of the self with the Divine. Some consider moksha to be an abode of paradise linked with one of the gods of Hinduism such as Vishnu or Shiva. Personal identity remains in this paradise. With the ultimate goal of moksha or liberation in mind, Hinduism provides pathways to achieve that goal. Since human beings vary in significant ways in terms of temperament and abilities, a variety of pathways can lead to liberation. These pathways are described as *yogas* (disciplines or yokes that unite one with the ultimate). Three major yogas developed: *karma marga* (the way of works); *jnana yoga* (the way of knowledge or insight); and *bhakti yoga* (the way of devotion).

KARMA MARGA

The way of works, karma marga, is an ancient way that stresses rituals and rites in daily and communal life. Sacrifice to the gods is important, as is hospitality and service to others. Various codes of law, as the ancient *Code of Manu* and other customs, shaped traditions that defined the person's role in society and the rules therein to be followed. Family structure and male/female relations are clearly outlined. Similar to many old and current traditions around the world, women have little independence; their role was largely that of serving the men in their lives. The custom of *suttee* (sati), now outlawed, directed the wife of a deceased husband to throw herself alive on the funeral pyre of her husband. Such an act was one of high virtue. The life of a widow in India can still be very difficult.

JNANA YOGA

Jnana yoga, the way of knowledge or insight, grows out of the claim that ignorance is the major cause of the suffering and misery in human life. It is ignorance that is the basic human problem, not sin or moral failure. For the gifted, there is a discipline that can lead to insight that finally grants release. Various methods of reflection and meditation have been prescribed as a means of gaining such insight. Insight gained is not that of mere knowledge of fact or theory but of an immediate experience of deep truths. The goal is to *experience* directly the identity of self and the divine, of atman and Brahman. Such insight frees one from the trials of life. The entire universe is experienced as an expression of God who is All. Joy is to be found in giving, not in getting. The highest good is achieved by way of renunciation, by giving up attachment to the things of the illusory world. Such is a Hindu version of the Truth that sets you free.

BHAKTI YOGA

Bhakti yoga, the way of devotion, came onto the scene about the time of Jesus and is now the most widely traveled pathway in India. It is a way for the common man or woman who has neither the time nor inclination to gain philosophical knowledge. It is a way free from the need for sacrifices. It is a way of heartfelt devotion to one of the gods chosen from the list available in Hinduism. Bhakti yoga brought with it a more celebrative attitude toward embodied existence. The body can joyously express itself as a temple of some chosen deity. Emotions can be expressed instead of being controlled through meditation and other disciplines. Ecstasies can be legitimately experienced in this world. Reflecting the general mood of toleration in Hinduism, the followers of bhakti yoga do not deny the efficacy of the way of knowledge or the way of works. They do, however, maintain that the way of complete devotion to a deity is an appropriate and effective pathway to salvation. The Hindu devotional classic, the *Bhagavad Gita*, elevates the way of devotion when Krishna, one reincarnation (avatar) of Vishnu, urges Arjuna to cling to him with heart and mind. The great promise of release will be fulfilled when Arjuna clings with trust to Krishna. Some Hindus suggest that Christianity is a striking form of bhakti yoga with Jesus—as an incarnation (avatar) of Krishna—being the object of devotion and trust.

SOME PERMISSIBLE LIFE GOALS: PLEASURE, SUCCESS, DUTY

Western views of Hinduism often focus on thin holy men in minimal garb at holy sites as the image of Hinduism. However, reflecting the pattern of diversity within Hinduism, there are permissible goals in life other than asceticism in quest of moksha. Pleasure (*kama*), especially through lovemaking, is one permissible goal. Hinduism has long affirmed the joy of sex and offers a manual to be of aid in the quest, the *Kamasutra* (love manual). A "natural law" view of morality in Hinduism might suggest that since sexuality is such a dominant part of existence, pleasure can be seen as one of the natural aims of sex—not just reproduction. This pleasure seeking, however, should always be kept within the bounds of standard social rules. While pleasure is a permissible goal, the individual will come to realize that there are goals more significant and deeply satisfying than pleasure.

Another permissible goal is what current culture in the United States might call success (*artha*). This is the goal of power, wealth, and social status. A great king might serve as a model for such a goal. Hindu writings on this topic grant that this can involve toughness and ruthlessness. As with kama, however, the individual finally learns that success is not the highest goal to pursue. A higher permissible goal would be *dharma*, a religious moral law that shows the pathway to a deeply satisfying life. The model would be the outstanding citizen of a community, someone who honors the duties linked to family, caste, and community.

THE FINAL GOAL: MOKSHA

As deeply satisfying as dharma may be, it is not to be seen as the final and most complete goal. The final and most satisfying goal is moksha—salvation, liberation, release. This is release *from* the sufferings that come with life and *from* the cycles of reincarnation. This is also a release *to* the bliss of union with the Divine, a union which is beyond description by mere human language. Release may be reached by any of the various yogas described earlier.[6]

THE IMPACT OF BRITISH COLONIALISM

The contrasts between the Christian story and the Hindu story are striking. In addition to these contrasts, various Hindu responses to the story brought by Christian missionaries were also complicated by the presence of colonial power.[7] The British East India Company had contacts with India as early as 1612. To protect its interests, the Company developed its own military, which was made up largely of recruits from within India. After a major rebellion in 1757, the British Government nationalized the Company and administered the enterprise, including its armed forces. The British ruled until Indian independence in 1947. While there may have been Christian churches in India as early as the sixth century, serious dialogue between Christians and Hindus came with British colonial activity. Since British power ruled India, the Christian missionaries no doubt felt empowered and had the primary goal of critiquing and overcoming Hinduism.[8] A more respectful dialogue developed later in history.

CHRISTIAN MISSIONS

Early British missionary activity was reflected in the work of Baptist William Carey, who arrived in Calcutta in 1793 and died in India in 1834. His work is of special interest because of his interest in social reform and his work in translations. By the time of his death, his mission had translated the entire Bible or parts of it into many languages and dialects. He also translated

Hindu scriptures from Sanskrit to English so that his fellow countrymen could become familiar with the material. This missionary activity naturally called for a response by Hindus to Jesus's question, "Who do people say that I am?" (Mark 8:18) In the face of the twin challenge of Christian missions and British colonialism, Hindus sought not only to clarify their identity as Hindus but also to maintain self-respect in the face of a European culture that assumed a superior attitude.

HINDU RESPONSES TO THE CHRISTIAN STORY

Aside from accepting the full Christian message—converting to Christianity—Hindus had several alternative responses. One response was to reject Jesus and his teachings outright. Another response was to reject the Christian doctrines *about* Jesus. Still another was to fold Jesus into the Hindu story in a way that did not betray basic Hindu beliefs. Many responses deserve to be heard, but a limited number of representative voices will be presented: Dayananda Saraswati (1824–83), Ram Mohan Roy (1771–1833), Ramakrishna Paramahamsa (1836–86), Swami Vivekananda (1863–1902), and Mohandas Karamchand Gandhi (1869–1948).

SARASWATI'S CRITIQUE OF THE CHRISTIAN STORY

A number of major Hindu voices were generally positive toward the figure of Jesus as a teacher, but they rejected the Christian message *about* him. This approach was expressed by Dayananda Saraswati. He sought to undercut the Christian story by claiming that only ignorant and credulous peoples can believe that Jesus was born of a virgin and that he performed miracles of healing. Such stories, he argued, are in conflict with the laws of nature. Consistent in his views, Saraswati also rejected similar accounts of miracles from Hindu traditions as mythological. He viewed Jesus as completely human, a rather simple and ordinary man without any significant knowledge or power, but also a man who shared universal values. Saraswati's view reflected his strong sense of Indian nationalism that developed out of his resistance to both Christian missionary activity and British colonial power.

RAM MOHAN ROY AND REFORM HINDUISM

More positive Hindu responses to Jesus reflect a spectrum that ranges from those who saw Jesus as a teacher of rational and universal values to those who embraced him as another incarnation of God. An influential figure who held that Jesus was a teacher of rational and universal values was Ram Mohun Roy (1772–1833). His education included the study of Hinduism,

Buddhism, Zoroastrianism, Islam, and Christianity, all of which led him to reflect a position similar to Enlightenment figures of Europe. His developed views reflected Deism and the Unitarianism of that day. While he viewed all religions as partially flawed human attempts to relate to the Divine, he urged the unity of all religions and proposed to find that unity in similar moral pathways. Roy founded a reform movement in Hinduism, the Brahmo Samaj, which had both social and religious elements, including the issue of women's rights. He opposed the caste system, child marriage, and the practice of suttee—the burning of the widow on the funeral pyre of her husband.

For Roy, the significance of Jesus was that of a teacher of universal values that are at the core of all great religions—once these religions are cleared from what he deemed as irrationalities and superstitions. Themes within Christianity that Roy rejected include the doctrine of the Trinity, Christ's death as atonement for sin, and Jesus as an incarnation of God. In pursuit of social reform, leaders in the Brahmo Samaj also rejected several basic Hindu beliefs, including karma and reincarnation. Those two beliefs were crucial foundations in support of the caste system that Roy rejected. In many ways, Ram Mohan Roy's views are very similar to those of Thomas Jefferson, a contemporary of Roy halfway around the earth. If a "large tent" view of Christianity is needed to include Jefferson, a "large tent" view of Hinduism may also be needed to include Ram Mohan Roy. How much of classical Hinduism can a person reject and still be considered a Hindu? This question can also be applied to all great religious stories.

RAMAKRISHNA: JESUS AS *AVATAR*

In contrast to Ram Mohan Roy, several Hindus accepted Jesus as an incarnation (avatar) of God. One such influential figure was Ramakrishna Paramahamsa (1836–86). His followers look upon him as a great guru as well as an incarnation of God. For Ramakrishna, religious faith is best practiced in intense experiential forms. He might correctly note that deep religious *experience* always trumps rational arguments. Deep mystical experienced shaped his own religious convictions.

One mystical experience came upon him one day while he contemplated a painting of the Madonna and Christ. The experience led him to the belief that he had realized his unity with Christ just as he had realized his unity with other figures such as the goddess Kali, and Muhammad. The Goddess Kali was a center of his own devotional life. He looked upon Jesus as one who is in eternal union with God and is the Master Yogi. Jesus is love incarnate. While Ramakrishna believed that Jesus was an incarnation of God, he did not believe that Jesus was uniquely so. Others, such as the Buddha and Krishna, were also incarnations. On the basis of his mystical experiences with a great variety of religious figures, he came to believe that all religions are pathways to the Divine. Religious mystics often seem led to the conclusion that there is an Ultimate Unity and Harmony in all things. In modern times, this impulse may be reflected in the quest of physicists for a Grand Unifying Theory that can link the basic forces in the universe.

SWAMI VIVEKANANDA AND RELIGIOUS UNITY

This urge to find a basic unity in all religions was forcefully expressed by a famous pupil of Ramakrishna. This figure was Swami Vivekananda (1863–1902), founder of the Vedanta Society in New York City. His participation in the World's Parliament of Religion, held in Chicago in 1893, helped to make him an influential voice. Vivekananda was an admirer of a book about the life and teachings of Jesus, *The Imitation of Christ* by Thomas à Kempis, a Roman Catholic monk. On the other hand, Vivekananda was highly critical of many missionaries who knew nothing about the people of India, could not speak their language, and lived in segregated communities insulated from the people of India.

In pursuing his view of the basic unity of religions, Vivekananda held that Hinduism should be honored as a world religion, just as Judaism and Christianity are so honored. Furthermore, he taught that God could be found in Jesus of Nazareth—but not only in Jesus. God can be found in the great voices that came before Jesus and after him, and similar voices are also to come in the future. Such a vision is clearly expressed in the *Bhagavad Gita*, the Hindu classic that was a favorite of Vivekananda. A moral vision directed his life. He held that unselfishness is the ideal of morality and that Jesus's teachings centered on just such an ideal.

MOHANDAS GANDHI: JESUS AS TEACHER

No survey of Hindu views of Jesus of Nazareth could be complete without the inclusion of Mohandas Gandhi (1869–1948), revered by many as the father of the nation of India. Following in the steps of Roy, Ramakrishna, and Vivekananda, Gandhi supported a view of the basic unity of all religions. He also hoped not only for an independent nation of India but also for an Indian society that was inclusive of a variety of faiths—Hinduism, Islam, Christianity, and others. He reported that his early view of a Christian was of someone with a bottle of brandy in one hand and a meal of beef in the other. Later, after reading the Sermon on the Mount (Matthew 5–7), his impression of the faith—if not that of the presumed faithful—changed. That Sermon not only became the whole of Christianity for Gandhi but was also what endeared him to Jesus. Gandhi's developed view of the policy of non-violence grew largely from his reading of the Sermon on the Mount and also from the writings of Leo Tolstoy, the Russian author who was also deeply influenced by the teachings of Jesus.

Gandhi came to believe that Jesus was one of the greatest teachers who ever walked this earth, but he also believed that Christian doctrine about Jesus as the *only* son of God leads to a misunderstanding of the message of Jesus. Christian *talk* about the Incarnation and the atonement tends to lead Christians away from the *walk* that Jesus emulated. Gandhi's reading of the Sermon on the Mount helped inform his view that religion cannot be divorced from politics. Justice and mercy are what love pursues in the world.

Gandhi's non-violent approach to solving human disagreements helped in his quest to free India from the rule of Great Britain. Somewhat paradoxically, his success in this venture led to his violent death at the hand of a Hindu nationalist, Nathuram Godse, who believed that Gandhi had betrayed his nation when Pakistan was separated from India. "Godse bowed to Gandhi reverentially before shooting him to death, and Gandhi raised his hand in a gesture of forgiveness as he fell."[9] That gesture of forgiveness might be seen as one of the most "Christian" of actions possible. The gesture may also be seen as a tribute Gandhi was willing to pay to Jesus, one of the world's Great Men—although for Gandhi, not the sole Great Man.

NOTES

1. For developed presentations of Hinduism see A. L. Basham, *Origins and Development of Classical Hinduism* (New York: Oxford University Press, 1989); David Noss, *History of the World's Religions*, 12th edition (New York: Prentice Hall, 2007); and Arvind Sharma, "Hinduism," in Arvind Sharma, editor, *Our Religions* (New York: HarperCollins, 1993).

2. Daniel Boorstin, *The Discoverers* (New York: Random House, 1983), 566.

3. The opening lines of the creation myth in Genesis 1 suggest that God created the universe out of some kind of original chaos. This has some affinity with an earlier Babylonian creation myth that told of a gigantic struggle between opposing powers or deities. In the Genesis story, there is only one deity. The Greek philosopher, Plato, suggested that a "world maker" (not "God") used some available material to form the world. According to Plato's account, the material world is faulty in a number of ways because the original material used was inferior. Even for Plato the material things of this world are only "shadows" of the truly Real.

4. There are a variety of views about nature of the resurrection. For distinctions within the New Testament writings, see E. P. Sanders, *The Historical Figure of Jesus* (London: Penguin Press, 1993), 276 f.

5. This cultural musical form is described in William Barrett, *Irrational Man: A Study In Existentialism* (New York: Doubleday Anchor Books, 1962), 54 f.

6. These four permissible goals have a close resemblance to the "stages on life's way" described by Danish philosopher Soren Kierkegaard: aesthetic, moral, and religious. For Kierkegaard, the first two stages lead to despair. Only the religious stage provides an adequate answer to the anxieties of the human venture.

7. Swami Vivekananda wrote that the East India Company sought to keep missionaries out of India and that the Hindus were the first to welcome some of the early missionaries. See Gregory Barker and Stephen Gregg, *Jesus Beyond Christianity: the Classic Texts* (New York: Oxford University Press, 2010), 179.

8. Chakravarthi Ram-Prasad, "Hindu Views of Jesus," in Greg A. Barker, editor, *Jesus in the World's Faiths* (Maryknoll, NY: Orbis Books, 2005), 83.

9. Arvind Sharma, *Our Religions* (New York: HarperCollins, 1993), 3.

Chapter Six

Jesus in Buddhism

Although generally classed as one of the great world religions, certain factors suggest that Buddhism is a *philosophy* rather than a religion. This suggestion grows out of several basic features of the original story: (1) the absence of anything like a God; (2) the denial of a human soul independent of the human body; (3) no claim to revealed truth or revealed scriptures; and (4) no role in the story for a law-giver to guide the faithful or a figure who redeems human beings from a sinful condition. Buddhism claims to be grounded in human experience and rationality, not in divine authority. Its central aim is to provide a practical *answer* to the problem of suffering, not a speculative system designed to explain the *origins* of suffering—like the story of the Fall in Christianity. Whether Buddhism is a religion or a philosophy, there are a range of Buddhist responses to the Christian story. Before reviewing these responses, the central teachings of the Buddhist faith will be described.[1]

THE BIRTH STORY OF THE MAN WHO BECAME THE BUDDHA

Somewhere around 560 BCE, a child was born who eventually became one of the Great Men of history.[2] This child was named Siddhartha Gautama and later attained the title of the Buddha—the Enlightened One or the Awakened One. The Buddhist story tells of his birth as a prince in India. His mother died shortly after his birth. A diviner foretold that the child would become either a great ruler or a significant religious figure. Preferring that his son become a great ruler, the father raised his son in princely fashion and sought to keep him away from anything that might incline him toward religion. As the child matured, his father shielded him from the harsher aspects of human life. Siddhartha married a devoted wife, and they had a son, Rahula. (The name appears almost prophetic since it means "fetter" or "impediment.") In his twenties, Siddhartha was living what seemed to be an ideal human life at that time in history.

GROWING ANXIETIES

Yet, as the story develops, the young father experienced a growing dissatisfaction and unease. In the weeks to follow, the "four passing sights" deepened his distress. The first of these sights was that of a sick person the young prince saw as he went riding beyond his sheltered environment with his charioteer. This was, as the story goes, the first time he had ever seen a diseased person. The next tour exposed him to the sight of an old person; again, the first time he had seen an old person. The third passing sight was that of a corpse, seen for the first time. The fourth passing sight was that of a wandering holy man who had left his family and was seeking liberation from the sufferings of life. There may be a deeper meaning to the phrase "for the first time" when applied to these four passing sights. In this deeper sense, he really *discerned* sickness, old age, and death "for the first time." He realized not only the problem of human suffering but also the need to find an answer to the problem. He had moved beyond the psychological state of denial and *saw* these painful aspects of the human venture.[3]

THE SEARCH FOR A SOLUTION

Deeply troubled by the four sights, human suffering became an intractable dilemma for Siddhartha. He was neither ill, nor old, nor near death, yet he found himself suffering in their shadows. His life of leisure and wealth seemed empty of meaning, and he found no adequate guidance to his unease in the Hinduism of his day. At the age of twenty-nine, he left his sleeping wife and child, rode away from home, shaved his head, took off his fine garments, donned a simple robe, and set off in search of a healing solution to the problem of suffering. For six years he studied and experienced various religious pathways of the India of his day. A period of severe asceticism left him emaciated and near death. Finally, he vowed to find a middle path between the asceticism of some holy men and the plush pleasures of his early life.[4] Sitting under a tree in Bodhgaya, India, he focused on the problem. After forty-nine days, the Buddhist story continues, he arrived at crucial insights. He became "awakened." He realized that all things undergo change, that nothing is permanent, and that we suffer because we wish that things were different. From that insight he became the "Light of Asia."[5]

THE MIDDLE PATH AND THE FOUR NOBLE TRUTHS

After his awakening, the Buddha decided to share his insights with others. This first took place in a deer park in North India, where he delivered his first sermon to five men who had shared his attempts at asceticism before he sought the Middle Path. The sermon consisted of the Four Noble Truths: (1) To live is to suffer (*dukkha*).[6] (2) Suffering is caused by desire or ignorant craving (*tanha*). (3) Suffering can be overcome. (4) Suffering can be overcome by following the Noble Eightfold Path.

This eightfold path includes: right view, right intention, right speech, right action, right livelihood, right effort, right mindfulness, and right concentration.[7] The Path leads to the goal of *nirvana*, the ultimate state of release from suffering. "Nirvana" can be translated by "fire going out" or "blowing out." The image suggests both the cessation of suffering and the cessation of craving. It also implies a peace and bliss that cannot be described by mere human language. To *experience* nirvana is to *know* its meaning. The sermon identified the problem, explained its origin, and presented a practical solution.

SOME BASIC BUDDHIST BELIEFS

Any attempt to condense Buddhist teachings into a few brief paragraphs fails to do justice to a subtle and complex tradition that took on modified forms as it moved throughout Asia. Nevertheless, such an attempt must be made in order to understand Buddhist reactions to the Christian story. While the Buddha focused on a practical pathway to nirvana and avoided pointless philosophical speculations, he did express some deep convictions about the human situation. Central convictions of the Buddha would include his views regarding God or the gods, the concept of *annica* (impermanence), the concept of *anatta* (no self), and modified views on the law of *karma* and *samsara* (rebirth).

Just as most Hindus of his day, the Buddha believed that there were gods, goddesses, and other nonhuman agencies, but he rejected belief in some eternal Being or transcendent Reality. While the Buddha granted that there may be gods and other agencies, these were finite, subject to death and rebirth, and were of no help in the quest of nirvana. This implied his rejection of Hindu scriptures and the role of priests who were members of a high caste. Buddhism is seen as heretical by devout Hindus because of its rejection of the role of priests and the Hindu scriptures. The Buddha also rejected the caste system.

Chapter 6

BUDDHIST ANTHROPOLOGY: NO SELF

Just as gods are transient entities, so are human beings. The Buddha rejected the widely held view that human beings have a central self or soul that has existence independent of the body. For the Buddha, there is no "I" who *has* a body or inhabits a body. This view is in stark contrast to Plato's view of the body as the "prison house" of the soul and that the soul is released from this prison at death. Instead, for the Buddha, this sense of an individual *self* is an illusion to be set aside. Just as a candle flame has no inner reality beyond the flame as a process, so human beings are a flowing process of physical and conscious dimensions. We *are* that process. The process involves change and eventually death. This self is also an aspect of the impermanence of all things. All is process, change, impermanence.

Death is an aspect of the process, and at death the process goes on in other forms. But there is no *self* that goes on to inhabit another body. The analogy of a candle flame may be suggestive. The flame from one candle can ignite a flame in another candle. But the new flame is *not* the *same* flame as the flame that was the igniting source. Both flames are processes. The process is related to the law of karma in that karma—resulting from good or evil deeds—is carried over in death and rebirth. This process continues until the bad karma is removed through following the eightfold path to Nirvana. With the achievement of Nirvana and its implied wisdom, the person has overcome ignorant craving. With the cessation of craving, the cycle of rebirth is ended. In the achievement of Nirvana, the fires of desire have been "blown out," the karmic consequences have ended, and there is no longer a rebirth. Peace at last.

Given his view of anatta (no self), Buddha's views regarding karma and samsara (rebirth) seem obscure. The law of karma represents a form of cosmic justice—a person gets what he or she deserves by way of reward or punishment in the next life. Bad karma accumulated in one life carries over as a burden or punishment into the next life at rebirth. Justice suggests that the *person* who receives this punishment must be the *same person* who performed the karmic-laden deeds. But the doctrine of anatta appears to deny this continuity of a "self" (or soul) from one life into the next. If there is no meaningful sense of a "self" that carries over into the next life after rebirth, then the consequences of karma would appear to be empty. Buddhist scholars have wrestled with that problem in a variety of ways. As they wrestled with the issue, they sought to preserve not only the concept of anatta but also some meaningful sense of karma and rebirth.[8] The subtleties of this problem run beyond the scope of this work.

EARLY BUDDHIST CRITICISMS OF THE CHRISTIAN STORY

This brief summary of Buddhism reveals the sharp contrast to the Christian story. We would expect, then, some sharp criticisms of the Christian story by Buddhist voices. Since Buddhism had a long history of competition and conflict with both Hinduism and Islam, their scholars were well versed in defending their faith against rival stories. Two types of defenses were raised against Christianity. One defense was to show that Christian faith and doctrine were logically and factually faulty. The second defense was to fold the figure of Jesus securely within the Buddhist point of view while rejecting Christian doctrine *about* Jesus. Since Buddhists made no claim to revealed truths, they shaped their defense largely through what they deemed as logical arguments and common sense. Given the imperialism of European Christian powers, Buddhist reactions to Christianity were often linked to the negative impact of this imperialism.

CRITICISMS BY FABIAN FUCAN, JAPANESE

An early criticism of Christianity came from Fabian Fucan (ca.1565–1621), a Japanese convert to Christianity through Jesuit missions.[9] While a Christian, he actively defended his new faith against Buddhism, Confucianism, and also Shintoism. When he later left the Christian faith—perhaps because the Church refused to ordain him—he turned his arguments against the Christian story. His attacks were aimed largely at Christian doctrine by questioning, for instance, why a merciful God would postpone the atonement for some five thousand years after the fall of Adam and Eve. During all those years, human beings were evidently falling into Hell while this God watched and seemed not to care.

Fucan also noted that the Christian view of the history of the earth—some six thousand years since creation—was considerably shorter than that recorded by Chinese and Japanese historians. The lifelong virgin status of Mary and Joseph ran counter to what Fucan held to be a universal moral law that defined the proper role of man and woman in the perpetuation of humanity. Fucan also concluded that the crucifixion of Jesus by the Jews was quite proper since he had made claim to being Lord of Heaven and Earth. Because the Christian story was wicked to the core and contradicted the wisdom of various sages, Fucan held that Japanese rulers were justified in using violence against the menace. This violence was largely a reaction by Japanese warlords to Spanish imperialism. Christianity was seen as a disease brought to Japanese shores by a foreign and evil power.

CRITICISMS BY OUYI ZHIXU, CHINESE

A systematic criticism of Christianity was formulated by a Chinese Buddhist monk and scholar, Ouyi Zhixu (1599–1655), who described the Christian story as incoherent. His criticisms were aimed primarily at Christian *doctrine* about God and the atonement, not at the person of Jesus. One of his attacks echoes the persistent problem of the presence of evil in the creation. He notes that Christianity proclaims not only that God is all-good and all-powerful, but also that there *are* evils in the world and evil spirits active in the world. But the presence of such evil indicates that this creator God cannot be all-good and all-powerful.

Zhixu also argued that the doctrine of the incarnation was incoherent, since it is clear that if God is the Absolute, then he cannot be born as a human being. He rejected the doctrine of the forgiveness of sin by way of the divine sacrifice of God's own body by maintaining that this forgiveness could have been made directly without such a sacrifice. Another criticism echoes charges that were made against the Apostle Paul. According to Zhixu, if God buys human beings free from their sins by way of an atoning sacrifice, then it suggests that human beings can sin without any concern for consequences.[10] Zhixu concludes that the Christian story is not only incoherent, but it also relieves human beings of their moral responsibilities.

A BUDDHIST FOLK-TALE ABOUT JESUS

One way of attacking a competing religion is to construct a counternarrative that undercuts the competitor's story by pointing out evil aspects of the founder.[11] Such a counternarrative is expressed in a Sinhalese Buddhist folk tale recounted around 1762 during the Dutch colonial period in Sri Lanka. The story about Jesus and his followers is an attack on Christian colonizers of the time and reflects the bitterness of those oppressed. Jesus is portrayed as a demon in disguise, and his followers are described as drunken meat-eaters who steal from others. The story holds that after Jesus was decisively killed and securely buried by soldiers of the king, some forces of evil gathered at the grave and proclaimed that the one in the grave was born again and had ascended into heaven. However, the people of the area inspected the grave and found it intact. The heretic son of the carpenter was securely dead and buried. The story ends with the hope that the Sinhalese people will again live securely in their land with Buddhist faith.

THE BIRTH STORY OF JESUS INCLUDES A BAD OMEN

In 1873, during a debate between a Buddhist monk and a Sinhalese Methodist clergyman, the monk presented a series of charges against Christianity. He noted that, while there were many very positive omens that occurred at the birth of the Buddha, there was a very bad omen that accompanied the birth of Jesus. His reference was to the massacre of the innocents by King Herod recorded in Matthew's Gospel. The monk considered this massacre to be an omen indicating that Jesus was an imposter who came into the world intending to send everyone to Hell. The monk also claimed that it was quite clear that Jesus did not rise from the dead but that his followers took his body away at night.[12]

MORE POSITIVE ATTITUDES TOWARD THE TEACHINGS OF JESUS

The passage of time may help to heal old wounds and produce more moderate voices. An example of such a voice was Anagarika Dhamapala (1864–1933), who gained acclaim for his participation in the World's Parliament of Religion in Chicago in 1893. He is a national hero for Sri Lankan people because of his support for Buddhism in Sri Lanka and because of his resistance to British rule. His education in Christian schools in Sri Lanka led him to value some of the teachings of Jesus; however, he viewed the God of the Old Testament as a tyrannical deity. Dhamapala is another example of a non-Christian scholar who rejects much of traditional Christian doctrine *about* Jesus, but finds in the teachings of Jesus much to affirm.

> I would suggest to ignore the stories of the O.T. as divine scriptures. As folklore stories of a nomadic people we should treat the Old Testament. The pure teachings of the gentle Nazarene we have to sift from the later theological accretions, and then we can make Jesus a central figure in the universal church of truth.[13]

Dhamapala considered that some of teachings in the Sermon on the Mount reflect universal application and showed parallels to the teachings of the Buddha. However, he did not consider the teachings of Jesus to be particularly sublime and thought of Jesus as a man with limited knowledge. He criticized Jesus's parable of the sower, for instance, because it reflected little knowledge of agriculture. A wise farmer would know better than to sow seed on rocky ground. (Matt. 13:3–9) While the Buddha taught ethics that human beings could apply to their lives, Dhamapala thought that some of the teachings of Jesus were impossible to follow. He also argued that anyone who would send persons to an eternal hell because they failed to believe that he was the son of an Old Testament God could not be considered either wise or merciful.

BUDDHISM AS THE SUPREME WISDOM

Buddhists often reflect a persistent—and legitimate—pride in their history of discipline, scholarship, and practical wisdom, but Buddhist scholars, like those of other traditions, sometime display an element of condescension toward other faiths. A Chinese scholar-monk, Sheng Yen (1930–2009), voiced this attitude. He held that the Buddha was naturally superior to others because of his superior education and the royal palace environment in which he was raised; moreover "his powers of understanding were exceptional." On the other hand, Jesus was raised in a small town, of a lowly family, and with little education. The Buddha taught for many years and at times before a gathering of over one thousand eminent monks. Jesus, in contrast, while extremely appealing, spoke only to a few people and for a limited number of years. This limited background and superficial knowledge hindered Jesus whose emotions conquered his reason. "Jesus grew up in a poor and lowly environment, preached his doctrine in a poor and lowly environment, and from amidst a poor and lowly environment headed towards a poor and lowly crucifix—to be crucified at Golgotha between two thieves!"[14]

THE DALAI LAMA'S VIEW OF JESUS

In contrast to Sheng Yen, a deeply appreciative attitude toward Jesus as a teacher is reflected in the words and works of Tenzin Gyatso, the 14th Dalai Lama (1935–). Since his exile from Tibet, he has become a very popular figure in the West not only because of his emphasis on the basic compatibility of moral themes in world religions, but also because of his charm and simplicity. For many, he exudes Buddhist nature. He writes of the good heart of Jesus reflected in the Sermon on the Mount where Jesus emphasizes tolerance, patience, and love—even for enemies. The Dalai Lama notes that some of these passages could be placed in Buddhist writings and not even be recognized as Christian.[15] While he expressed high regard for Jesus, he did not hold anything like the Christian view that Jesus was unique. "For me, as a Buddhist, my attitude toward Jesus is that he was either a fully enlightened being or a bodhisattva of a very high spiritual realization."[16] True to his own Buddhist story, the Dalai Lama accepts a Jesus that folds into that Buddhist story while declining to accept traditional Christian doctrine about Jesus. The Dalai Lama reflected intellectual honesty by acknowledging that Christian doctrine is quite different from Buddhist thought. In contrast to some modern Hindu thinkers, he has not encouraged a mood of religious unity. He does, however, believe that a moral unity could be discovered in the teachings of Jesus and Buddhism.

THICH NHAT HANH: BUDDHIST-CHRISTIAN PARALLELS

Another influential Buddhist figure in the United States is a Vietnamese Zen monk, Thich Nhat Hanh (1926–).[17] Two of his books published in the 1990s were best-selling works on Buddhism: *Living Buddha, Living Christ* (1995) and *Going Home: Jesus and Buddha as Brothers* (1999). In contrast to the Dalai Lama, Thich Nhat Hanh not only points out many similarities between Christianity and Buddhism, but also develops interpretations designed to show that the two share identical themes. Buddhist mindfulness is a counterpart to the Christian view of the Holy Spirit. God and Nirvana are both references to what theologian Paul Tillich called "the ground of being." The Christian doctrine of the resurrection is another way of speaking about reincarnation.

While Hanh has an image of Jesus and an image of the Buddha in his home altar, Jesus has his place on that altar because Hanh sees Jesus through Buddhist eyes. This is reflected in Hanh's suggestion that Christians should replace representations of Jesus on a cross for ones that portray him in some meditation pose.[18] He also rebuked Pope John Paul II for holding that Jesus was "absolutely unique" and "the one mediator between God and humanity." These claims, Thich Nhat Hanh observes, reflect an "attitude that excludes dialogue and fosters religious intolerance and discrimination."[19]

When the Christian story comes into contact with the Buddhist story, competition between the followers of two Great Men comes into play. To retain their faith identity, Buddhists must show that their Great Man, the Buddha, is greater than the Jesus of Christianity. This is accomplished, as noted above, by either diminishing the stature of Jesus and his teachings, or by reframing Jesus in Buddhist terms and folding him into the Buddhist story. The Buddha is affirmed as the greatest of Great Men.

NOTES

1. This work attempts no adequate description of the complexities of the Buddhist story, which is modified in various ways as it moved throughout Asia. For helpful works on Buddhism: John S. Strong, *Buddhisms: An Introduction* (London: Oneworld Publications, 2015), and David Noss, *History of the World's Religions*, 12th edition (New York: Prentice Hall, 2007).

2. This period in history is known as the Axial Age, when many significant figures came upon the scene worldwide. These would include Confucius in China, Zoroaster in Persia, Mahavira (Great Man) founder of Jainism, early Hebrew prophets, and early Greek philosophers. These Great Men helped to shape much of ensuing world history.

3. After a grandfather had died, a five-year-old child asked her grandmother, "Daddies don't die, do they? They have us little kids." Around the age of ten, children generally become

aware that they, too, will die. This is also often the age when religions induct their children into their traditions.

4. The severely ascetic teachings of Jainism developed in India from the teachings of Mahavira (599–527 BCE). Tradition holds that after years of asceticism, he died from voluntary self-starvation and become victorious over the cycles of reincarnation.

5. *The Light of Asia: The Great Renunciation*, by Sir Edwin Arnold, published in 1879.

6. "Dukkha" has a variety of possible translations: "pain," "sorrow," "suffering." Some modern scholars use "stress." In this work, "suffering" is the chosen translation because "stress" seems too weak to carry the weight of the problems of sickness, old age, and death.

7. For an exploration of these paths, see John S. Strong, 147 f.

8. A helpful discussion of these concepts can be found in John S. Strong, *Buddhisms: An Introduction* (London: Oneworld Publications, 2015), chapter IV.

9. See Gregory Barker and Stephen Gregg, *Jesus Beyond Christianity: The Classic Texts* (Oxford: Oxford University Press, 2010), chapter IV for readings that inform this chapter.

10. Paul addresses this issue in his letter to the Romans: "What then are we to say? Should we continue in sin in order that grace may abound?" (Romans 6:1)

11. Peter Schäfer maintains that portions of the Jewish Talmud construct just such a counternarrative against Jesus. See Peter Schäfer, *Jesus in the Talmud* (Princeton: Princeton University Press, 2007).

12. Gregory Barker and Stephen Gregg, 239 f.

13. Anagarika Dharmapala, "An Appreciation of Christianity," in Gregory Barker and Stephen Gregg, 242. It should be noted that most of the above criticisms were written before New Testament scholars retrieved the "historical Jesus." No contemporary New Testament scholar would refer to Jesus as a "gentle Nazarene" speaking softly in that ancient world.

14. Gregory Barker and Stephen Gregg, 253–4.

15. This view can move in both directions. A guest preacher in a Christian church once read—as *scripture* for the day—portions from Buddhist writings that echoed New Testament passages regarding love. Later in the service he acknowledged the source and linked it to his sermon. The congregation responded with interest to the message.

16. The Dalai Lama, *The Good Heart: A Buddhist Perspective on the Teachings of Jesus* (Boston: Wisdom Publications, 1996), 83.

17. Stephen Prothero, *American Jesus: How the Son of God Became a National Icon* (New York: Farrar, Straus and Giroux, 2003), 287-9.

18. This shift in imagery can be found in many Protestant churches where the image of Jesus as the Good Shepherd replaces images of the crucifixion.

19. Thich Nhat Hanh, *Living Buddha, Living Christ* (New York: Putnam, 1995) 193.

Chapter Seven

Jesus Only?
Religions and the Fate of Others

Which religion—or non-religion—are you betting on? This is a question philosopher Blaise Pascal (1623–1662) might have asked. The question reflects his *wager* approach to religious faith. Pascal claimed that neither religious faith nor atheism could be established on purely rational grounds. Both positions are beyond the conclusions of evidence and logic. Nevertheless, he continued, human beings must choose one or the other since no decision would be, in effect, denying religious faith. We live by one belief or the other. Since a decision must be made, how is it possible to decide?

Pascal suggested that the problem should be seen as a type of wager. Is religious faith or is atheism a better bet in terms of possible loss and possible gain? He thought that during their time on earth, both atheists and those of religious faith could have equally happy lives. There would be no great advantage in either while alive, but the final consequences are monumentally different. If you bet on atheism and you are right, then dead is dead. But if you bet on atheism and you lose, then you face eternal damnation. On the other hand, if you bet on religion and are wrong, you lose little since dead is dead. But if you bet on faith and are correct, you gain eternal glory. With much to gain and nothing to lose, religion is the most rational wager. "If you gain, you gain all; if you lose, you lose nothing."[1]

Some may object, Pascal noted, that God will not honor a faith stance that was merely the result of a wager. In response, he suggested that in order to achieve genuine faith the seeker should observe the way of believers. "Follow the way by which they began; by acting as if they believed, taking the holy water, having masses said, etc. Even this will naturally make you believe and deaden your acuteness."

WAGER ON WHICH RELIGION?

Currently, Pascal's *wager* could be expanded to include a great variety of major world religions as well as various cults and sects that have emerged around the planet. Questions remain: Which religion holds the most promise for a potential believer? Which religion guards against the most severe loss? Granted, there is no objective evidence or argument that can confirm the truth of any of the major faiths. Religious faith remains *faith*, not *knowledge*. Furthermore, there are no conclusive arguments that favor atheism. Religious faith and atheism are both life commitments that run beyond *confirming* arguments or evidence.

This chapter explores how various religions view the ultimate fate of individuals who follow a faith pathway different from their own. If faith is a form of life investment, what is the nature of promised return or loss? The focus will be on beliefs regarding life after the death of the body. With the possible exception of Buddhism, all the religions discussed in this book teach that their pathway holds the promise of victory over death and a blissful existence beyond the death of the body. In the following discussion, "salvation" will be the general term indicating rescue from a death with negative consequences.

Firmly held religious convictions appear to be supremacist. Believers hold the conviction that they are privileged in some way and that their beliefs are the most promising life pathway. Religious language reflects this supremacist view in such terms as "the elect," or "the enlightened," or "the chosen," or "the straight path." None of the religions traced in this work have settled for a second-place rank in the religious competition. The supremacist claim especially underlies those religions that are missionary in nature—Christianity, Islam, Buddhism, and also Judaism at certain points in history. But the claim of all great religions is that their particular story is a fulfilling one—perhaps the uniquely fulfilling one.

Serious religious belief has deep emotional overtones. "You shall love the Lord your God with all your heart, and with all your soul, and with all your strength, and with all your mind." Parallel passages can be found in all great religions. Since religious belief is about the very meaning of life, it carries heavy emotional weight. Given this weight, the supremacist mood of the great religions brings with it the tendency to react negatively to a challenging religious story. Negative reactions to challenging beliefs range from condescending dismissal of the other story to various forms of violent attack on the "other." Religions also represent powerful forms of human tribalism.

It should be of no surprise to find hostile and demeaning references aimed at a challenging faith. A full range of voices from various religions will be explored in order to suggest a possible need for "truth and reconciliation" on the religious scene. The dark sides of traditions need to be addressed as well as the more positive elements. This dark side of religious stories often becomes manifest in the views of the ultimate fate of other believers. Believers are inclined to hate those deemed as hated by the believer's God. Or perhaps the God of a believer tends to hate those who are hated by the believer.

Given a supremacist claim by a religious faith, a question to those believers quite naturally arises: What is the fate of those who do not belong to your particular story and do not walk your pathway of faith? This question can be answered in several ways. *Exclusivists* hold that their faith is not only supremacist, but it is also the only final pathway to salvation. This exclusivist position can be expressed in two forms. *Rigid exclusivists* hold that all non-believers are destined for Hell and will remain in Hell eternally. Rigid exclusivists also believe that passages in their sacred texts which assert exclusivist views should trump any passages which might qualify that position. *Soft exclusivists*, on the other hand, hold that their faith is the only pathway to salvation; however, unbelievers may not be destined for an eternal Hell. Instead, God's mercy may provide not only for a temporary stay in Hell for a "cleansing" of the soul but also for an opportunity after death to attain the true saving pathway.

Inclusivists hold that theirs is the True Path to salvation; nevertheless, sincere believers of another faith may also attain salvation. The soft exclusivist position may be thought of as an inclusivist view. *Pluralists* hold that there are a variety of religions that can lead to salvation. This position is sometimes expressed as "All roads that lead to God are good." On the face of it, however, that affirmation may be empty of significance since it leaves open the question of whether or not a particular road *does* "lead to God." Roads that truly lead to God could be viewed as good, but it may be that not all faith roads *do* lead to God. Neither exclusivist position would endorse this pluralist view. Finally, *universalist*s maintain that there is no permanent hell—all human beings are eventually saved.[2] Some soft exclusivist voices are also universalists.

In exploring answers to the question of the fate of others, a word of caution must be issued. There are a variety of voices in *each* of the traditions to be examined. Hinduism and Buddhism appear to be open to universalism. Voices from each of the monotheist faiths (Judaism, Christianity, and Islam) range all the way from rigid exclusivist to tolerant inclusivist and even universalist. The debate in all three faiths is open since there is no controlling authority. As Vatican II illustrated, debate is also expressed in the Catholic Church. What follows are some possible answers that are either clearly stated in the faith tradition or appear to be implied by the main beliefs expressed in the tradition.

HINDUISM ON THE FATE OF OTHERS

Hinduism's answer would appear to be straightforward. The human body is mortal and will die, but the essential self or soul (*atman*) continues to exist. All persons are caught up in the cycle of rebirth (*samsara*), and the nature of that rebirth is shaped by the law of karma. Past deeds shape the nature of your future embodied existence. Unless a person has attained release from the cycle of rebirth (*moksha*), that person will eventually be reborn in some fashion. In the meantime, there can be an intermediate state before rebirth. There are a variety of hells in Hinduism to which a soul might be subjected after death. These serve as appropriate cleansing or punishment in the cause of justice. While some texts speak of an eternal hell where some souls are trapped and are deprived of rebirth, the general view in Hinduism is that these hells (or heavens) are temporary. Eventually, the soul must again experience rebirth at the level appropriate to accumulated karma. The quest for release continues.

The goal according to the Hindu story is that of *moksha*—release from karmic fate and the cycle of rebirth. One direct implication of this story is that no human being will ever be finally shut out of that release just because they failed to be a Hindu in their lifetime. Release is open to all. Another implication is that all individuals will be caught up in the reincarnation cycle, reflecting the law of karma, until they follow an appropriate pathway leading to release. Within Hinduism, there are a number of yogas or pathways that enable the individual to gain that release. In this sense, only Hindus are "saved" or "released" since a prescribed Hindu pathway is required. Hinduism reflects a soft exclusivist view. In principle it is possible for everyone to eventually become a Hindu, pursue an appropriate pathway, and achieve release. The way of *bhakti yoga*, the way of devotion, may be just such an adequate pathway in Christianity when expressed as total devotion to Jesus as a divine incarnation. In this way the Christian may attain release, but the pathway is Hindu in its interpretation. Jesus is folded into the Hindu story. To accept the view that Christianity in its classical formulation is an adequate road to either salvation or release would be to reject a supremacist Hindu position. No Hindu voice explored in this work reflected such a view.

BUDDHISM ON THE FATE OF OTHERS

Buddhism parallels the Hindu position in many ways. Failing to be a Buddhist during a lifetime does not imply that the person is forever shut out of Nirvana. On the other hand, Buddhism appears to claim that the ultimate pathway to release is the Buddhist pathway. All others are faulty in some way unless they incorporate the Buddhist solution. This position is implied in the Buddha's rejection of the Hinduism of his day and also in the missionary nature of Buddhism. Linked to Buddhist views of karma and rebirth are concepts within Buddhism of various levels of heavens or hells. A being is born into one of the levels on the basis of the karma accumulated in the previous life. These levels, however, are not viewed as permanent. Instead, they are forms of existence in the cycles of rebirth (*samsara*). Rebirth in other forms will eventually occur until the being achieves Nirvana and rebirth ceases.

Non-Buddhist pathways may help a being achieve a higher level of existence in the next rebirth, but the achievement of *Nirvana* requires the Buddhist pathway. "It is agreed across the Buddhist traditions . . . that Buddhism stands at the top, that only by following the teachings of the Buddha can one be finally liberated from suffering and rebirth."[3] That pathway is always open to the seeker. No one is turned away forever. Buddhism reflects both a supremacist attitude and a soft exclusivist view.

SHARED MONOTHEIST BELIEFS

The major voices in the three monotheistic religions—Judaism, Christianity, and Islam—differ from Hinduism and Buddhism in several significant ways. While there are differences within each monotheistic faith, all three *generally* teach that human beings are called to be obedient to the will of the one and only true God. Furthermore, individuals have only one lifetime on earth—no reincarnation—and will face an ultimate destiny of either Heaven or Hell. These three monotheisms also hold that the members of their faith are linked in special ways to all persons of that faith—the Chosen People, the Church, the Ummah. Some voices in all three believe that those who are not part of the true community of faith may be rejected by God at the last judgment. At this point it must be noted again that not all believers within each of the three faiths agree with the beliefs just listed. These disagreements will be explored as each faith is examined.

ISLAM ON THE FATE OF OTHERS

The Islamic view of the fate of others is rooted primarily in the Quran. A central message of the Quran is that the prophet Muhammad follows in the great tradition of God's prophets such as Moses and Jesus. Consistent with that claim, the Quran expresses views about death, God's judgment, and the world to come that are similar to those of Judaism and Christianity. The Quran clearly teaches that there is both Heaven and Hell. Heaven is described in the Quran as a place where the pleasures and joys of bodily life can be fully affirmed. The tortures possible in Hell are vividly described in many passages. The Quran has more passages that describe the alternative hereafters than any other holy book. God may be compassionate and forgiving, but his judgment on evil is certain, just, and frightening.

Within Islam there seems to be no clear line that can be drawn between those who get to heaven and those who do not. Khaled Abou El Fadl suggests caution when making claims about what Muslims believe. "Ultimately, the Qur'an, or any text, speaks through its reader. . . . Any text . . . provides possibilities for meaning, not inevitabilities. . . . If the reader is intolerant, hateful, or oppressive, so will be the interpretation of the text."[4] Abou El Fadl implies that scriptures are Rorschach tests. His observation may help explain the variety of views within Islam to be described.

VERSES FROM THE QURAN ON THE FATE OF OTHERS

1. "No; Abraham in truth was not a Jew, neither a Christian; but he was a Muslim and one pure of faith; certainly he was never of the idolaters. Surely the people standing closest to Abraham are those who followed him, and this Prophet, and those who believe; and God is the Protector of the believers." (3:60)
2. "Surely they that believe, and those of Jewry, and the Sabaeans, and those Christians, whosoever believes in God and the Last Day, and works righteousness—no fear shall be on them, neither shall they sorrow." (5:73)
3. "Surely the godfearing shall be in a station secure among gardens and fountains . . . They shall not taste therein of death, save the first death." (44:51)
4. "The unbelievers of the People of the Book and the idolaters shall be in the Fire of Gehenna [Hell], therein dwelling forever." (98:5)
5. "Whoso desires another religion than Islam it shall not be accepted from him; and in the next world he shall be among the losers. . . . God guides not the people of the evildoers" (3:79, 3:81)

Muslim scholars have pondered these various passages from the Quran and have offered a variety of interpretations of their meaning throughout history.[5] "God may be One, but Islam most definitely is not."[6] A number of widely held views have a long history if not complete agreement among Muslims: (1) Idolaters are destined for Hell. (2) Some souls will abide in Hell eternally. (3) Persons who reject Islam after first being part of the faith are destined for Hell. (4) Those who fail to become Muslims after learning and understanding the faith are destined for Hell. (5) Muslim sinners may be subjected to at least some time in Hell. (6) God will be the final judge in these matters showing both His mercy and His justice. (7) Persons truly submitted to the will of God (Muslims) are promised a blessed life in the Hereafter.

POSSIBLE MUSLIM PLURALIST VIEW

A brief case study of possible interpretations of the first passage from the Quran cited above (3.60) will illustrate contrasting views of such passages. That passage notes that Abraham was a Muslim—in the sense that he was submitted to God's will. As such, Abraham is clearly one who will be accepted into Heaven on the Day of Resurrection. This would also apply to a number of other Old Testament figures as well as Jesus. Some Muslim scholars hold that this passage expresses an inclusivist view in that some persons are clearly saved even though they could not have responded to the message of the Quran. These scholars further suggest that this passage implies that others might be saved even though they are not personally committed to the Muslim faith. Jews and Christians who are submitted to the will of God may also achieve salvation. Muslims expressing this view might be called *pluralists* by suggesting there are a number of possible salvation pathways apart from membership in the Muslim community. Nevertheless, the pathway described is that of submission to God—the central theme of Islam. This possible pluralist view might best be described as soft exclusivist.

A MUSLIM EXCLUSIVIST VIEW

In contrast to pluralist views, a Muslim scholar of the eleventh century expressed a *rigid exclusivist* view that Khalil considers to be so extreme as to be "bizarre."[7] Ibn Hazm (994–1064) claimed that Islam is the only path to salvation. Furthermore, anyone who had heard the Prophet's message but then rejected it is destined for Hell. In a sweeping assertion, he also held that all human beings had encountered the message of Islam in some way and were, therefore, culpable as unbelievers. There are two polar responses that exclusivist Muslims may have toward unbelievers. They may make sincere efforts to convert the unbelievers to save them, or they may "look down upon them as the damned—and treat them as such."[8] Exclusivists are not confined to any particular religious story. This Muslim view is mirrored in some Christian assertions that those who have not responded to the Christian message of salvation through Christ are destined for Hell. This could presumably include even those who have not heard the message of salvation through Christ.

THE INCLUSIVIST VIEW OF HAMID AL GHAZALI

A towering figure in the history of Islam, Abu Hamid Muhammad al-Ghazali (1058–1111), came to adopt an inclusivist view. He believed that Muhammad's message is the surest guide to salvation, but he also expressed a profound trust in God's abundant mercy.[9] During his own quest for a true faith, he observed that parents tend to have substantial influence on the beliefs held by their children. Children raised as Christian tend to remain Christian. Children raised as Jews tend to remain Jews. Children raised as Muslims tend to remain Muslims. Evidently parental efforts to induct their children into a tradition usually succeeded. From this observation, Ghazali concluded that all children are born with a "pure natural disposition" toward religious belief and that parents can shape the *content* of that belief. (This perspective is reflected in a flurry of current books that suggest that human beings have something like a "God gene.") Ghazali concluded that it was crucial for children to be directed to the true religion of Islam since all others contained grievous errors. A child may be born with a pure natural disposition toward the true God, but this can be blurred or tarnished by corrupted religious teachings coming from a child's elders.

Ghazali was puzzled by the fact that many persons rejected the Muslim faith—a message he thought was convincing not only because of the power of the message but also because of the miracles attributed to Muhammad. He believed that miraculous events showed the power and actions of God alone and confirmed the Prophet's mission. Convinced that Muhammad's message was the truly saving pathway, Ghazali pondered the ultimate fate of nonbelievers. The destiny of heaven or hell was at stake. Unbelievers, evidently, were destined for Hell. But this invites the question of what it means to be an unbeliever. It seemed clear that anyone who had clearly heard and understood Muhammad's message but chose not to believe could be classed as an unbeliever. But what of someone who had never heard the message? Or what of those who had heard only a warped or critical view of the message? Since the Quran apparently did not supply a clear and distinct answer to such questions, a variety of interpretations developed.

Ghazali's interpretation emphasized divine mercy over divine wrath and suggested that eternal bliss "will be the norm and eternal torment the exception."[10] Eternal torment would be for those who were truly unbelievers in that they *rejected* the message of Islam after hearing it in its "true" form. But others might be excused on several grounds. Some never heard of the prophet and his message, and others heard only a warped and defective message about Islam. These may be destined for a limited time in Hell in order to receive a punishment appropriate to their failings, but Heaven would be their final destiny. There were also those who encountered the message of Islam, investigated it thoroughly, and still did not affirm the faith. They may have inquired in earnest but suffered from a certain mental blindness. While they did not convert to Islam, this non-conversion was not to be seen as an outright denial or rejection. This category could open a wide door for inclusivists and allow some Jews and Christians into Heaven.

A MUSLIM UNIVERSALIST

Joining the ranks of exclusivist, inclusivist, and pluralist voices are the universalists. Since the Quran stresses that God is both thoroughly just and also compassionate, some Muslim scholars posit that God's compassion should be the dominant theme. This leads to the suggestion that while many deserve some time in Hell, justice cannot be served by condemning such sinners to an eternity in Hell. Both God's compassion and His justice can be served by a lighter sentence.

A fourteenth century figure who arrived at a universalist position and who had the title of "the master of Islam" was the scholar Taqi al-Din Ahmad Ibn Taymiyya.[11] In his fifties, this scholar wrote an extensive work designed to show that Islam was superior to both Judaism and Christianity and that all people should follow Muhammad and the revelations he received. Unbelievers of various kinds deserve God's punishment. Taymiyya claimed that anyone of sound mind and reason would come to understand that the message brought by Muhammad was true and should be followed. Anyone of sound mind who has heard the message but who does not accept it is worthy of being cast into Hell. Those who have not heard the message—the *unreached*—will be addressed by a messenger on the Last Day and will have an opportunity to respond at that time. Thus all human beings will have had an opportunity to become believers.

Near the end of his life, Taymiyya was given a commentary on the Quran written by an earlier Muslim scholar. The volume included a statement from Umar, a companion of Muhammad and second leader (caliph) of Islam after Muhammad's death. Umar evidently had suggested that Hell would not be eternal. This report led Taymiyya to write a lengthy work in which he argued that all punishment is temporal and that finally all human beings would be saved. In that work he refuted the view, held by some Muslims, that both Heaven and Hell are temporary. He went on to refute the view that both Heaven and Hell are eternal. His final position was that Heaven is, indeed, eternal but that Hell is not.

He arrived at that conclusion by citing a variety of passages from the Quran that supported such a view.[12] A key passage from the Quran (6:128) invoked by Taymiyya has God saying that the Fire is the destiny for some "*unless* God wills otherwise." In the end, God and only God will determine who is saved and who is not. This view allows the interpreter to emphasize

God's mercy over His wrath. Temporal punishment is an expression of mercy since it cleanses the guilty of sin; but there would be no mercy in a punishment that was eternal. God's merciful nature overrules an eternal Hell. In developing this conclusion, Taymiyya refutes a view held by some scholars that punishment in Hell is temporary because Hell eventually consumes—annihilates—these souls. In contrast, he holds that all souls in Hell will eventually become citizens of Heaven. Taymiyya voiced a soft exclusivist position.

It is no surprise that some future Muslim scholars repudiated Taymiyya's universalist position. The debate in Islam is still lively and charges of "unbelief" are sometimes leveled against the universalist view. Current voices in Islam still reflect the range of views from exclusivist to universalist. Perhaps all Muslims would agree that, in the end, only God decides who is saved and who is not. That view may be difficult for a Muslim to reject.

JUDAISM ON THE FATE OF OTHERS

The vast majority of books and essays about Judaism emphasize the diversity of thought in Jewish history. The model for this diversity is reflected in the Talmud which records lively debates among the rabbis as teachers of the Jewish people. God may be One, and the Torah may be revelation from God, but in Judaism no person or group can presume to speak exclusively for God. This diversity is reflected in the various current divisions within Judaism: Orthodox, Reform, Conservative, and Reconstructionist. Diversity within Judaism is also reflected in the quest for *normative Judaism*. "It is difficult to define such a norm due to the serious divergences among the modern Jewish religious streams. It is often easier to say what is not normative, rather than what is."[13] While it may be difficult to identify a normative Judaism, central themes in the history of Judaism would include God, Torah, and Israel. In keeping with the diversity within Judaism, a range of Jewish voices regarding the fate of others will be explored.

JUDAISM ON THE GENERAL FATE OF HUMAN BEINGS

Within the history of the people of Israel and emerging Judaism, differing views emerge about the fate of *human beings* in general. Except for some later materials, the Hebrew Bible (Old Testament) does not indicate any significant religious beliefs about individuals surviving death. The great Hebrew prophets, for instance, never threatened some kind of judgment after death as a means of encouraging the people to be obedient to God's will. These same prophets did threaten that consequences for disobedience would fall upon the Israelites within history. The focus was very much "this-worldly." God's concern was for the continuing existence of the *people* of Israel, not of individuals. Individuals may die, but the people live on. There are Biblical passages that allude to some type of shadowy existence in *sheol* after death, but death did not bring a closer relationship with God, nor did it result in punishments or rewards.

A differing view of the afterlife developed during the Babylonian Exile which took place after the defeat of the Southern Kingdom of Judah by the Assyrians (586 BCE). Historians generally believe that new views of the afterlife came into Judaism by way of the Persian religion, Zoroastrianism. That religion taught both the resurrection of the dead and the judgment before the High God bringing either punishment in some type of hell or a blissful life in heaven.

Belief in some world to come after death may also have been a means of defending the claim of God's justice since many great and good souls had died without anything like recompense in this world. Furthermore, justice would appear to require some type of punishment for evil persons who received no such penalty in this life. Specific persons who received this just punishment are mentioned in the Talmud. Belief in resurrection and judgment shifted the focus, in part, to the individual, but the significance of Israel as a people of God remained crucial.

By the time of Jesus, the party of the Pharisees in Judaism held to belief in the resurrection of the dead and of judgment before God in the World to Come. The opposing party of the Sadducees rejected both beliefs, but that party disappeared from history after the destruction of the Jerusalem Temple in 70 CE by Roman legions under Titus. After that catastrophe, the teachings of the Pharisees became dominant through the Rabbis who shaped the future of Judaism.[14] The highly influential Jewish philosopher, Moses Maimonides (1135–1204 CE), taught that both the resurrection of the dead and God's judgment are among the major principles of the faith.

Forms of mysticism have been expressed widely in the world religions, although mystics have sometimes professed theories that are suspect by more traditional believers and scholars. A mystical movement, the Kabbalah, developed in sixteenth-century Judaism and produced a variety of unusual views.[15] Some Kabbalistic thinkers expounded an elaborate view of human souls that included reincarnation. The movement reflected some philosophical themes rooted in Platonism. Lower levels of the soul could undergo punishment after death, while higher levels achieved a more glorious destiny. Some Kabbalistic thinkers suggested that reincarnation functioned as a means of punishment for sins but also granted another chance for glory. Still other Kabbalistic thinkers posited that both Jewish bodies and Jewish souls are essentially different from those of gentiles.[16] This difference would imply different destinies in the World to Come.

The idea of an immortal human soul, distinct from the physical body, is not reflected in Biblical writings or in the Talmud. An early clear view of this "body-soul dualism" is found in the works of the Greek philosopher, Plato (430–347 BCE). During the Enlightenment, this view moved into some Jewish circles and eventually became a standard position in Reform Judaism. The Pittsburgh Platform of 1885, ratified by American Reform Rabbis, rejected not only belief in the resurrection of the body but also belief in Heaven and Hell. The Platform also asserted that the human soul is immortal. A full-throated defense and presentation of this theory is presented in *Jewish Theology*, a 1923 work by Kaufman Kohler, then President of Hebrew Union College.[17]

Aside from the Orthodox community, contemporary voices in Judaism focus on this world—not on an anticipated afterlife. Early in the twentieth-century, Franz Rosenzweig (1886–1929) thought of eternity "as a religious dimension of life, not as an afterlife state." The absence of belief in God's retribution on evil persons in an afterlife made responses to the Nazi Holocaust particularly painful.[18] Hitler just died!?

JUDAISM AND THE FATE OF GENTILES

Just as a variety of beliefs have been expressed in Judaism regarding the ultimate fate of *all* human beings, a variety of Jewish beliefs about the ultimate fate of *gentiles*—all non-Jews—have also been expressed. In general, leading Jewish thinkers concerned themselves largely with the life of faith for the Jewish people living in a world where ruling powers were either Christian or Muslim. The major commitment is to walk in the world as God would have them walk. "He has told you, O mortal, what is good; and what does the Lord require of you but to do justice, to love kindness, and to walk humbly with your God?" (Micah 6:8) Nevertheless, three beliefs are basic: a fierce monotheism, the gift of the Torah from God, and serving as God's chosen people.[19]

While the major focus was that of being a people obedient to their covenant with God, the interaction of Jews with other belief systems would naturally raise the question of the ultimate fate of those who are *not* part of God's covenant with Israel. This question is explored in a debate attributed to sages in the Mishnah and Tosefta.[20] Eliezer says, "None of the gentiles has a portion in the world to come, as it is said, 'The wicked shall return to Sheol, all the gentiles who forget God' (Ps. 9:17)" Joshua, however, retorts that the Psalm quoted included the phrase "gentiles who forget God." He goes on to claim that this phrase implies that there are gentiles in the world who are righteous and will have a portion in the world to come.[21]

This leaves open the question of the standard by which a gentile might be considered to be "righteous." In response to this question, Jacob Neusner writes: "What makes a gentile righteous is that he does not forget God. But remembering God entails acknowledging him and that makes the gentile into an Israelite." Neusner develops his position on the basis of what he refers to as Classical Judaism—the Judaism reflected in the sages of the Talmud. That tradition, according to Neusner, defines gentiles (all non-Jews) as idolaters, enemies of God. "The upshot may be stated very simply. Israel and the gentiles form the two divisions of humanity. The one will die but rise from the grave to eternal life with God. When the other dies, it perishes; that is the end."[22] This reflects a rigid exclusivist perspective.

Other Jewish scholars reflect a more optimistic view of the fate of gentiles. George Robinson suggests that some non-Jews can be saved without becoming Jews. "It is said in Jewish lore that there will be a reward in the world to come for the righteous of all nations, and those who follow the Noahide laws."[23] Robinson does not comment on the fate of gentiles who fail to be righteous, although the implication seems to be that the "unrighteous" will *not* be saved. Robinson also notes that the view cited is "in Jewish lore." Neusner might ask, "At what point does *lore* have more authority that the sages of the Talmud?"

As noted above, Reform Judaism's Pittsburgh Platform of 1885 muted the issue of the fate of Gentiles by rejecting resurrection along with Heaven and Hell. The shift from resurrection of the dead to the immortality of the soul leaves open the question of the ultimate fate of the soul. Presumably gentiles also have immortal souls. If the scales of justice are to be balanced by way of reward or punishment after death, these sanctions would have to be worked out in *soul* terms, not the imagery of *bodily* bliss or pain. On the other hand, the shift to immortality of the soul could suggest a universalist view of salvation—all human beings would eventually be saved. This universalist view seems not to be conspicuously voiced in Judaism, although some positions within Reform and Reconstructionist Judaism may be open to this line of thought.

TALMUD ACCORDS THREE TO HELL

The Talmud (extended rabbinical commentaries on the Torah, completed by 600 CE) gives examples of persons appropriately assigned to Hell as sinners and enemies of Israel.[24] Titus, the Roman general who brought about the destruction of Jerusalem and the burning of the Jerusalem Temple, was—for good reason—considered to be one of the great enemies of Israel. Having been responsible for the burning of the Jerusalem Temple, the punishment given to Titus reflected his sin. His body is burned to ashes; the ashes are then shaped again into a body and burned again and again—for eternity.

Balaam was a non-Israelite prophet who aided the king of Moab to bring disaster to the Israelites by way of Moabite prostitutes and unclean food. (Numbers 22:1 f.) These offenses enraged God who sent a deadly plague upon the Israelites. Balaam was punished in Hell with boiling semen. The Tosefta's account suggests that Balaam was punished for some twelve months and then was erased from existence. Jesus the Nazarene, according to these accounts, was destined for an eternity in Hell similar to the fate of Titus. Jesus was evidently condemned for being one of the worst heretics to come out of Israel. His punishment is that of sitting in boiling excrement for eternity.

Scholars find nothing in the Talmud that provides any actual information about the Jesus of history. The accounts in the Talmud about Jesus appear to be a counternarrative to the Christian story about Jesus. This counternarrative asserts that Jesus was not resurrected from the dead but is sitting in Hell forever together with other sinners. This story also carries a warning to the followers of Jesus who face the same destiny. This story about Jesus reflected the hostile relations between Judaism and developing Christianity and functioned as a forceful attack upon a deviant faith story.

The debate and discussion within Judaism grants richness to the long tradition and reflects the changes brought about through various historical circumstances. The fate of the gentiles remains an open question in Judaism since no group or person has the last word. Confrontations between various supremacist faiths—such as Judaism and Christianity—always add tension to such issues.

CHRISTIANITY ON THE FATE OF OTHERS

With its consistent theme of "Jesus only," Christianity may rank as the most exclusivist faith among the major world religions. Islam has produced scholars with strong exclusivist claims; nevertheless, historical Islam has always looked with some tolerance on Judaism and Christianity. While the "Jesus only" theme dominates, the range of thought within Christianity on this issue is very broad. Strong inclusivist voices arrive on the scene, and universalist voices are also heard. At stake is the destiny of human beings—Heaven or Hell—after the death of the body [25]

DESTINIES: HEAVEN, HELL, PURGATORY, AND LIMBO

While the major alternatives for Christianity in the World to Come were those of Heaven and Hell, the Roman Catholic Church altered the scene by adding other possibilities. These additions attempted to deal with troublesome issues linked to the relationship between God's justice and God's mercy. God's justice prevails for those justly condemned to eternal Hell. These would include the unbaptized who died with original sin on their soul, and also those guilty of serious (mortal) sin that had not been effaced through sacraments and penance. But eternal damnation for those dying with less serious sins (venial) on their soul would seem to be unjust. Nevertheless, such souls are not yet ready for admission into Heaven. The Church formulated the doctrine of Purgatory as a temporary place of punishment and cleansing for these souls. As a place for cleansing, those in Purgatory are destined to be saved after a period of time that was needed for the effacing of the sins. After a period in Purgatory, Heaven would be assured. The doctrine of Purgatory was a major issue in the Protestant Reformation. Reformers Luther and Calvin held that the doctrine of Purgatory had no Biblical foundation. Furthermore, many voices within the Catholic Church in the sixteenth century complained that the doctrine led to corruption in the Church. Believers were told that by giving money to the Church they could reduce the time in Purgatory for dead loved ones. Indulgences were openly advertised to that end.

The concept of Limbo addressed the question of the ultimate fate of those who died without the sacrament of baptism—a sacrament required for the effacing of original sin. This would include persons who lived and died before the Church was founded and, therefore, had no access to baptism. It would also include children born in the Christian era but died before they were baptized. Such souls seemed to be barred from Heaven, but justice would not seem to require that they be condemned to eternal punishment. The concept of Limbo held that such souls would enter an appropriate Limbo where they would experience a "relative completion" if not the beatific vision of God.[26]

Purgatory is a doctrine that is affirmed and restated in the *Catechism of the Catholic Church*, 1995. Limbo is considered to be theological speculation and has never been an official doctrine of the Church. While Limbo is not mentioned by name, the *Catechism* states: "Regarding children who have died without baptism, the Church can only entrust them to the mercy of God." Furthermore, Jesus's tenderness toward children allows "hope that there is a way of salvation for children who have died without baptism."[27] These observations appear to imply that God's mercy is not necessarily bound by the limitations of the sacraments of the Church.

BIBLICAL FOUNDATIONS FOR CHRISTIAN SUPREMACY

The supremacist position of any religion is anchored in its own self-told story. These anchors are usually the scriptures accepted by that faith as revealed truths. The Christian supremacist story of salvation through the gracious gift of God in Christ is declared in several New Testament passages: "I am the way, and the truth, and the life. No one comes to the Father except through me." (John 14:6) "There is salvation in no one else, for there is no other name under heaven given among mortals by which we must be saved." (Acts 4:13) "For there is one God; there is also one mediator between God and humankind, Christ Jesus, himself human, who gave himself a ransom for all." (I Timothy 2:5) Since the documents containing these passages achieved the status of revealed Scripture, Christian writers are required to work out the implications of those claims. Christianity appears to be not only supremacist but also exclusivist.

IMPLICATIONS OF THE FALL OF ADAM AND EVE

The centrality of Christ for salvation is also linked to the story of the Fall of Adam and Eve as interpreted by traditional Christianity. That story, largely through the influence of Augustine, yielded the doctrine of Original Sin. According to this doctrine, the sin of these first human beings is passed on to each generation. As the Calvinist New England primers put it: "In Adam's Fall, we sinned all." In effect, every human being is *born* alienated from God, guilty of sin.

The Fall also left human beings in a state of depravity which rendered them unable to live the righteous life required by God's Law. Minds are darkened, and the will is crippled. Human beings not only begin as sinners, but they are also unable to do the good works which could make them acceptable to their Creator. Furthermore, this Original Sin can be forgiven only through the grace of God achieved through the death and resurrection of His Son. This view is expressed in the doctrine of the Atonement—the gracious act of God that brings humanity back into right relation with the Creator.[28]

This somber assessment of the human situation leads to the conclusion that hope for salvation is utterly dependent on the grace of God.[29] The "Good News" of the Christian story is that this grace is available as a gift through faith or trust in God. The diagnosed problem—sin— is overcome by the prescribed remedy—grace. For those who do not partake of the remedy, the result is eternal damnation.

While this exclusivist view of Christianity is expressed in the Christian New Testament, it is worked out in Roman Catholic and Protestant traditions in contrasting ways. With due respect to other expressions of Christianity, only these two traditions will be examined for the sake of brevity. Other Christian traditions reflect similar viewpoints.

THE ROMAN CATHOLIC CHURCH ON THE FATE OF OTHERS

Teachings of the Roman Catholic Church leave the impression that not only is Christian faith the only means of salvation, but also that the Catholic Church alone possesses this faith. This rigid exclusivist view is asserted in a number of Papal proclamations. Pope Innocent III (1160–1216) declared: "There is but one universal Church of the faithful, outside of which no one at all can be saved." In his Papal Bull of 1302, *Unam Sanctum* (One Holy), Pope Boniface VIII proclaimed: "We declare, we proclaim, we define that it is absolutely necessary for salvation that every human creature be subject to the Roman Pontiff." This position was asserted by Pope Pius IX (Pope 1846–78): "On the ground of the Faith it is to be firmly held that outside the Apostolic Roman Church none can achieve salvation. This is the only ark of salvation."

A catechism for children repeats this imagery of the saving ark: "How thankful I am to be a Catholic. I belong to the Church which Christ founded on the Apostles. The Church is the ship of Peter. As long as I stay on the ship I will be safe. If I get off it, I will be drowned."[30]

Later in his statement, Pope Pius IX qualifies the claim: "In the same manner, however, it must be accepted as certain that those who suffer in invincible ignorance of the true religion, are not for this reason guilty in the eyes of the Lord."[31] That qualification *may* hold out the possibility of salvation for some outside of the Church—a soft exclusivist view.

SACRAMENTS AS THE MEANS OF GRACE

An exclusivist position is worked out in the life of the faithful through the sacraments of the Roman Catholic Church, which are not only the *signs* of grace but also the *means* of grace. These sacraments bestow grace that forgives sins, including Original Sin, and strengthens one for the Christian life. Some sacraments establish a reality, such as the sacrament of marriage. The effect of a sacrament comes *ex opere operato*—directly by the sacramental act itself. The act achieves that which it states. The sacramental effect is achieved regardless of the sanctity of the priest or minister who administers the sacrament. The priest or minister may be a sinner, but the sacrament administered is still valid. The effect of the sacrament also depends on the proper disposition of the recipient. Outside the Church, neither the sacraments nor the grace they confer are available to a human being. This sacramental theology appears to suggest that all human beings not part of the Catholic Church are lost sinners and are bound for Hell. Catholic theologians have, however, suggested that God's grace has other avenues of aid for such sinners.

This apparently exclusivist doctrine raises a variety of questions: What of the fate of others who claim to be Christians—Protestants, for example—but who are not in the Catholic fold? What of the fate of those who have never heard of the faith? Are they in their ignorance condemned? Catholic theologians have wrestled with these questions. Two issues appear to be at stake: (1) A rigid exclusivist position strikes many persons—inside and outside of the Church—as both narrow and arrogant. (2) Is it possible for the Church to change its view on this matter without undermining its claim of being a Truth that does not shift with the times? In response to the charge of narrowness and arrogance, any historian could note that all the great world religions are supremacist—if not exclusivist—at the core. Supremacist claims appear to constitute the nature of religion. Various claims are central to faith stories: "the straight path," "the enlightened," "the elect," "the chosen people." Those outside the circle of faith may judge these supremacist claims to be disrespectful if not disdainful.

It is, however, possible for a religion to be supremacist without being rigid exclusivist. The faith may claim to be the True religion, but it may also grant that those not of the True faith may eventually be saved by God's mercy. Hell, for instance, may eventually be emptied of residents. Some Muslim scholars have been both supremacist and inclusivist in that way. The question within Catholicism appears to be whether the Church can maintain its exclusivist claim but also hold a more inclusivist vision.

The issue of the ultimate fate of those who claim to be Christians, but not in the Catholic fold, is a persistent issue for Catholic thinkers at this point in history. The Second Vatican Ecumenical Council (Vatican II) held in Rome between 1962 and 1965 resulted in documents that addressed the fate of non-Catholics as well as non-Christians. The language of these documents is carefully worded, and the theologically uninitiated may find it difficult to arrive at a confident understanding of just what is being asserted.[32]

The official Catechism of the Catholic Church does not reject "separated" churches such as Protestants. "All who have been justified by faith in Baptism are incorporated into Christ; they therefore have a right to be called Christians, and with good reason are accepted as brothers in the Lord by the children of the Catholic Church."[33] The Catechism suggests, as well, that non-Christians may also find salvation—a soft exclusivist view.

> Those who, through no fault of their own, do not know the Gospel of Christ, or his Church, but who nevertheless seek God with a sincere heart; and, moved

by grace, try in their actions to do his will as they know it through the dictates of their conscience—those too may achieve eternal salvation.[34]

The documents suggest that God's saving grace *may* be available outside the Church for those who seriously seek God. The destiny of those who do *not* seek God appears to be dark. "The teaching of the Church affirms the existence of hell and its eternity. Immediately after death the souls of those who die in a state of mortal sin descend into hell, where they suffer the punishments of hell, 'eternal fire.'"[35] While conservative voices within the Church worried about Vatican II, the Council achieved some elements of *aggiornamento* (updating, modernizing) as Pope John XXIII had hoped. Language during debates—which included such terms as "evolving" and "progressing"—revealed something of the mood of those assembled.[36]

PROTESTANT CHRISTIANS ON THE FATE OF OTHERS

Early Protestant views of the fate of others were expressed by Reformers Martin Luther and John Calvin. In keeping with Scripture and the Catholic Church of their day, they asserted that *only* through Christ can salvation be achieved. While the church as a community of believers was important to these Reformers, the role of the church in the drama of salvation differed from that of Roman Catholicism. In Catholicism, the role of the Church was essential since it was only in and through the Church and its sacraments that God's saving grace could be found. For Luther, Calvin, and most other Protestants, the sacraments of Baptism and the Eucharist signify or *proclaim* God's grace but do not in themselves *confer* such grace. For Protestants generally, grace is viewed as Divine favor—God's love—made manifest in the life, death, and resurrection of Jesus Christ. Salvation is by grace alone (not of works) and by faith alone—trust in God. Some refer to this concept as the "cat-hold" view of faith. Mother cat (God) saves her child by picking it up by the nape of the neck and carrying it to safety. The kitten (Christian believer) just trusts in its mother (God).

The foundational claims in Protestantism were *sola scriptura, sola fide, sola gratia* (scripture alone, faith alone, grace alone). Protestants also affirmed the classic Christian creeds which speak of the resurrection of the body, not the immortality of the soul. But with the resurrection comes judgment. Committed to the authority of Scripture, traditional Protestants along with Catholics affirmed the reality of Hell or Heaven as the final destiny for human beings. Protestants omitted Limbo and Purgatory since they found no Biblical bases for such doctrines. The Protestant message was quite exclusivist, although it did grant that saving faith in Christ was not necessarily linked to any particular church or sect. Roman Catholics were not necessarily shut out of the World to Come provided that these Catholics trusted in God's saving grace instead of the sacraments of the Catholic Church. In other words, this salvation is to be understood in Protestant terms, not Roman Catholic.

THE DOCTRINE OF PREDESTINATION

The affirmations of faith alone and grace alone implied a form of *predestination*. Augustine was the first to develop this doctrine. Because of Adam's fall, all human beings are totally lost in sin. Human beings are saved by faith alone, but only God's grace can *enable* true faith. God's gift of grace is irresistible, but it is given to a limited number of persons. All others perish. This doctrine of predestination is nuanced in a variety of ways but was affirmed in some form by Thomas Aquinas, Martin Luther, and John Calvin. Calvin held to the harshest position by his doctrine of double predestination—that Heaven is God-ordained for some and eternal damnation is ordained for others. The Catholic Church rejects double predestination but grants the possibility of election to Heaven.[37]

This general exclusivist position of "Jesus only" has its difficulties. The Christian story holds that God is just, but God is also loving and merciful. Hell may be a form of God's justice, but an eternal Hell seems to call into question God's love and mercy. This tension between justice and mercy is reflected in Roman Catholic thought in reference to "the *mystery* of reprobation." And John Calvin deemed his doctrine of double predestination as a "horrible decree." Both God's justice and God's love must be affirmed, but only God knows how these are finally related. The existence of this apparent tension laid the groundwork for more inclusivist claims.

ORIGEN: AN EARLY UNIVERSALIST

Origen (185–254 CE) resolved this tension by asserting that Divine Love has the last word. Scripture may refer to God's justice and wrath, but it also speaks of love and mercy. For Origen, the scripture passages that emphasis God's love trump the wrathful passages. Origen opts for the universal salvation for all human beings. There may be a temporary purging of souls, but there is no permanent hell for anyone. The Catholic Church condemned Origen's position in the sixth century.

Later voices calling for a totally inclusivist view developed within the Protestant spectrum. Free from the opposition of a Church or a Pope, they could make their case from a scriptural perspective. This, of course, leaves open the possibility of heresy—if heresy remained a meaningful charge. In tracing the early debate between traditional exclusivists and emerging inclusivist views, it becomes clear that both sides could muster scriptural passages to defend their position. As referred to earlier, it appears that scriptures represent a Rorschach test of sorts. Readers appear to find in the scriptures the portions that reflect their own convictions. Those who moved toward a universalist position, wherein all are eventually saved, elevated the message of Divine love over that of the wrath of God.

PROTESTANT UNIVERSALISTS

The theological scene in the last three centuries has included a growing universalist position. An early figure was the Englishman John Murray (1741–1815) who founded the Universalist church in America. New Hampshire-born Hosea Ballou (1771–1822) was also an influential voice in the Universalist movement. Both men moved away from the harsh Calvinism of their early years. The highly influential Swiss Reform theologian, Karl Barth (1886–1968), had universalist leanings although he did not state the position clearly. A growing chorus of voices has suggested that God has no permanent problem children.

Universalists generally maintain the classical view that God is all-good, all-powerful, and all-knowing. Given those basic convictions, the problem of evil arises. If God is all-good, all-powerful, and all-knowing, then God would not *want* evil to exist, would have the *power* to eliminate evil, and would *know* how to eliminate evil. Yet evil exists. This problem deepens, argue the universalists, if Hell is asserted to be an eternal abode for some of God's created creatures. Universalists suggest that only if God's love ultimately prevails over evil can God be seen as all-good. An eternal Hell would stand in witness against God's love. Hence, God's love will prevail, and all will eventually be saved. Philosopher John Hick (1908–2012) expressed a soft exclusivist viewpoint:

> We must therefore assume that God's love continues to be active towards us in and through a series of aeons until at last we see the divine goodness and respond in glad adoration. This process, in which the infinite resourcefulness of infinite love will sooner or later find a way to us, depends upon the fact that it is God who has created us and that he has created us for himself. . . . It is because "our hearts are restless until they find their rest in thee" that in the end, however far off that end may be, human nature will arrive at its own self-fulfillment in a right relation to God.[38]

There are, to be sure, more conservative positions still strongly asserted in various circles of the Christian faith. This chapter has briefly examined how the Roman Catholic Church has reframed a rather traditional position during and after Vatican II. *Conservative* Protestant positions are expressed in several denominations. These conservative positions usually include the hard exclusivist claim that salvation is through Jesus Christ only, and at the judgment, the unsaved will be consigned to an eternal Hell.[39]

This hard exclusivist position remains as *one* telling of the Christian story that challenges voices expressing a more universalist view.[40] Exclusivists and universalists—alike—maintain their positions are firmly rooted in scripture. Although there is some discernable movement toward tolerance and universalism, the history of Christianity suggests that disagreements will continue. Perhaps theologians and other believers may find that universalism is more of a "win-win" strategy than is the more conflict-prone exclusivist position.[41] Who will finally be saved? A modest conclusion would suggest that *God only knows*.

The same modesty could be appropriately expressed regarding the judging of Jesus. This work has attempted to explore how various world religions have responded to Jesus's question, "Who do people say that I am?" The religions by which the faithful live have responded to the Christian story of Jesus in a variety of ways: He has been loved. He has been reviled. He has been carefully merged within other faith stories. All responses represent *faith* commitments, not matters of *knowledge* since the responses move beyond what fact or logic can confirm. That Jesus once existed is largely beyond doubt. But *Who* he was remains a major issue. Again, the modest—but faithful—response could be: *God only knows*.

For those who reject belief in God, Jesus's question may be only of historical interest. Some atheists may find significance in his moral perspectives; but since Jesus believed in God, he evidently suffered from what Richard Dawkins would call "the God delusion." Dawkins would no doubt concede that, in Jesus's day, the God delusion was widely shared and was not yet strongly challenged by science or philosophy.[42]

NOTES

1. Blaise Pascal, *Pensees*, Translated by W. F. Trotter. (New York: The Modern Library, 1941), 81.

2. For these distinctions, see Mohammad Hassan Khalil, *Islam and the Fate of Others: the Salvation Question* (New York: Oxford University Press, 2012), 7. Khalil argues that the rich diversity of views in Islam has been too long overlooked and needs to be appreciated at this time in history.

3. Gregory Barker and Stephen Gregg, *Jesus Beyond Christianity* (New York: Oxford University Press, 2010), 271.

4. Khaled Abou El Fadl, *The Place of Tolerance in Islam* (Boston: Beacon :Press, 2002), 22–23.

5. Ibid. This work is a comprehensive study of the question.

6. Reza Aslan, *No God but God: The Origins, Evolution, and Future of Islam* (New York: Random House, 2005), 263.

7. Khalil, 23.

8. Ibid., 25.

9. For an exposition of Ghazali's views see Khalil, 26 f.

10. Khalil, 40.
11. Ibid., 74 f. for a full development of his position.
12. Ibid., 81 f, for Taymiyya's argument.
13. Sarah E. Karesh and Mitchell M. Hurvitz, *Encyclopedia of Judaism* (New York: Checkmark Books, 2008), 359.
14. For a helpful review of Jewish views of death and afterlife, see Harold Coward, editor, *Life after Death in World Religions* (Maryknoll, New York, 1997), chapter one.
15. One historian maintained that the "Zohar-kabbalah is heresy of the most pernicious kind." Paul Johnson, *A History of the Jews* (New York: Harper Perennial, 1987), 199.
16. See Israel Shahak and Norton Mezvinsky, *Jewish Fundamentalism in Israel* (London: Pluto Press, 2004), 57 f.
17. Kaufman Kohler, *Jewish Theology: Systematically and Historically Considered* (New York: The Macmillan Co., 1923).
18. Harold Coward, 27.
19. The *Shema* is a central prayer in Jewish services and is presented in Deuteronomy 6:4 as the words of Moses: "Hear O Israel: The Lord is our God, the Lord alone." In its context, the prayer reflects henotheism—the belief that other gods may exist but loyalty belongs to one god. A fierce monotheism (there is only one god) develops later in the Hebrew Bible and carries over into Judaism.
20. The Mishnah and Tosefta are anthologies of laws attributed to Jewish sages from the period of 0–200 CE. The Mishnah eventually becomes part of the Talmud which was completed around 600 CE.
21. , See Jacob Neusner and Bruce Chilton, editors, *Religious Tolerance in World Religions* (West Conshohocken, PA: Templeton Foundation Press, 2008), chapter five. See also, Gary Porton, *Goyim: Gentiles and Israelites in Mishnah-Tosefta* (Atlanta Georgia: Scholars Press, 1988), 87–88.
22. See Jacob Neusner and Bruce Chilton, 200. Neusner notes that some Jews take up a differing position regarding Christianity and Islam since these faiths hold to monotheism. (216).
23. George Robinson, *Essential Judaism* (New York: Pocket Books, 2000), 175. Noahide laws refer to those given to Noah and his family after the Flood and are considered to be laws that apply to all human beings.
24. See Peter Schäfer, *Jesus in the Talmud* (Princeton New Jersey: Princeton University Press, 2007), chapter 8, "Jesus Punishment in Hell." Schäfer considers this material about Jesus to be "a most graphic and bizarre story about Jesus' descent to and punishment in hell." (83)
25. For a comprehensive study of various views of the World to Come, see Alan Segal, *Life After Death: A History of the Afterlife in the Religions of the West* (New York: Doubleday, 2004).
26. For a helpful guide to these various concepts, see Van A. Harvey, *A Handbook of Theological Terms* (New York: Macmillan Company, 1964.)
27. *Catechism of the Catholic Church* (New York: Doubleday, 1995). See page 291 for a discussion of Purgatory, and page 353 for observations about unbaptized children.
28. Two major formulations of this doctrine were briefly described in chapter two of this work: the Satisfaction Theory linked to Anselm (1033–1109), and the Moral Influence Theory identified with Abelard (1079–1144).
29. The German Theologian, F. D. E. Schleiermacher (1768–1834) described religion as "the feeling of absolute dependence."
30. Edward J. Kelly, *Baltimore Catechism No. 1 with Development* (Boise, Idaho: The Roman Catholic Diocese of Boise, Idaho, 1946), 78–79.
31. Ludwig Ott, *Fundamentals of Catholic Dogma*, Patrick Lynch, translator (St. Louis, Missouri: B. Herder Book Company, 1954), 310.
32. For works that explore Vatican II and its results, see: John O'Malley, *What Happened at Vatican II* (Cambridge, Massachusetts: The Belknap Press of Harvard University Press, 2008), and Adrian Hastings, editor, *Modern Catholicism: Vatican II and After* (New York: Oxford University Press, 1991).
33. *Catechism of the Catholic Church* (New York: Doubleday, 1995), 235.

34. Ibid., 244.
35. Ibid., 292.
36. John O'Malley, 196. For an excellent review of Catholic teaching in regard to the salvation of those outside of the Church, see Avery Dulles, "Who Can Be Saved?" *First Things*, no. 2 (2008).
37. See Van A. Harvey, *A Handbook of Theological Terms* (New York: The Macmillan Company, 1964) for helpful articles on these concepts.
38. For the developed argument, see John Hick, *God and the Universe of Faiths* (Oxford: Oneworld Publications, 1993), 70 f.
39. Explore statements by The Southern Baptist Convention, Liberty University, and Wheaton College, Illinois.
40. For the issue of universal salvation, see Robin A. Parry and Christopher A. Partridge, editors, *Universal Salvation: The Current Debate* (Grand Rapids, Michigan: Wm. B. Eerdmans Publishing Company, 2004).
41. See this theme in Robert Wright, *The Evolution of God* (New York: Little, Brown and Company, 2009).
42. Richard Dawkins, *The God Delusion* (New York: Houghton Mifflin Company, 2006).

Bibliography

Abou El Fadl, Khaled. *The Place of Tolerance in Islam*. Edited by Joshua Cohen and Ian Lague. Boston: Beacon Press, 2002.
Arberry, A. J. *The Koran Interpreted: A Translation by A. J; Arberry*. New York: Simon and Schuster, 1955.
Armstrong, Karen. *Muhammad: A Biography of the Prophet*. San Francisco: Harper Collins, 1993.
Aslan, Reza. *No God but God: The Origins, Evolution, and Future of Islam*. New York: Random House, 2005.
Bainton, Roland. *Christianity*. Boston: Houghton Mifflin, 2000.
Barker, Gregory, ed. *Jesus in the World's Faiths: Leading Thinkers from Five Religions Reflect on His Meaning*. Maryknoll, NY: Orbis Books, 2005.
Barker, Gregory, and Stephen Gregg, eds. *Jesus Beyond Christianity: The Classic Texts*. New York: Oxford University Press, 2010.
Bellah, Robert. *Religion in Human Evolution*. Cambridge, MA: Harvard University Press, 2011.
Berger, Peter. *The Sacred Canopy: Elements of a Sociological Theory of Religion*. New York: Anchor Books, 1967.
Blackmore, Susan. *The Meme Machine*. Oxford: Oxford University Press, 1999.
Boorstin, Daniel J. *The Discoverers*. New York: Random House, 1983.
Brown, Raymond. *An Introduction to the New Testament*. New York: Doubleday, 1997.
Bruteau, Beatrice, ed. *Jesus Through Jewish Eyes*. Maryknoll, NY: Orbis Books, 2001.
Burkett, Delbert. An *Introduction to the New Testament and the Origins of Christianity*. Cambridge: Cambridge University Press, 2002.
Catechism of the Catholic Church. New York: Image Doubleday, 1995.
Coward, Harold, ed. *Hindu-Christian Dialogue: Perspectives and Encounters*. Maryknoll, N.Y.: Orbis books, 1989.
Cragg, Kenneth. *Jesus and the Muslims: An Exploration*. Boston: One World, 1999.
Crossan, John. *The Historical Jesus: The Life of a Mediterranean Jewish Peasant*. New York: Harper, 1991.
Dalai Lama. *The Good Heart: A Buddhist Perspective on the Teachings of Jesus*. Boston: Wisdom Publications, 1996.
Dan, Joseph. *Kabbalah: A Very Short History*. New York: Oxford University Press, 2006.
Dawkins, Richard. *The God Delusion*. New York: Houghton Mifflin Company, 2006.
Ehrman, Bart. *The New Testament: A Historical Introduction to the Early Christian Writings*. New York: Oxford University Press, 2008.

Bibliography

Ellsberg, Robert, ed. *Thich Nhat Hanh: Essential Writings.* Maryknoll, NY: Orbis Books, 2001.

Esposito, John. *Islam, the Straight Path.* New York: Oxford University Press, 1991.

Frankfort, Henri. *Before Philosophy: The Intellectual Adventure of Ancient Man.* New York: Penguin Books, 1960.

Fredriksen, Paula. *From Jesus to Christ.* New Haven: Yale University Press, 2000.

Freedman, Harry. *The Talmud: A Biography.* London: Bloomsbury, 2014.

Gager, John. *Who Made Early Christianity? The Jewish Lives of the Apostle Paul.* New York: Columbia University Press, 2015.

Gaustad, Edwin, and Leigh Schmidt. *The Religious History of America,* rev. ed. San Francisco: Harper, 2002.

Goldstein, Morris. *Jesus in the Jewish Tradition.* New York: Macmillan, 1950.

Hanh, Thich Nhat. *Living Buddha, Living Christ.* New York: Riverhead Books, 1995.

Harris, Mark. *The A to Z of Unitarian Universalism.* Lanham, MD: The Scarecrow Press, 2003.

Harvey, Van. *A Handbook of Theological Terms.* New York: Macmillan, 1964.

Hick, John. *God and the Universe of Faiths.* New York: St. Martin's Press, 1973.

Jenkins, Phillip. *The Many Faces of Christ.* New York: Basic Books, 2015.

Johnson, Paul. *A History of the Jews.* New York: Harper and Row, 1988.

Katz, Jacob. *Exclusiveness and Tolerance: Jewish-Gentile Relations in Medieval and Modern Times.* Oxford: Oxford University Press, 1961.

Khalidi, Tarif, ed. and trans. *The Muslim Jesus.* Cambridge: Harvard University Press, 2001.

Khalil, Mohammad Hassan. *Islam and the Fate of Others.* New York: Oxford University Press, 2012.

Kohler, Kaufman. *Jewish Theology.* New York: The Macmillan Co., 1923.

Kraemer, Joel. *Maimonides.* New York: Doubleday, 2008.

Kung, Hans. *Islam: Past, Present and Future.* Oxford: One World Publications, 2007.

Laqueur, Walter. *The Changing Face of Anti-Semitism: From Ancient Times to the Present Day.* New York: Oxford University Press, 2006.

Levine, Amy-Jill. *The Misunderstood Jew.* New York: HarperCollins, 2006.

Maimonides. *Rambam: Selected Letters of Maimonides.* Translated and annotated by Avraham Yaakov Finkel. Scranton, PA: Yeshivath Beth Moshe, 1994.

Meacham, Jon. *American Gospel: God, the Founding Fathers, and the Making of a Nation.* New York: Random House, 2006.

Neusner, Jacob, editor. *God's Rule: The Politics of World Religions.* Washington, D.C.: Georgetown University Press, 2003.

———— *Introduction to Judaism.* Louisville, KY: Westminster/John Knox Press, 1991.

Neusner, Jacob, Alan Avery-Peck, and William Green, editors. *The Encyclopedia of Judaism.* New York: Continuum, 1999.

Noss, David. *History of the World's Religions.* New York: Prentice Hall, 12th edition, 2007.

O'Malley, John W. *What Happened at Vatican II.* Cambridge, Massachusetts: The Belnap Press, 2008.

Ott, Ludwig. *Fundamentals of Catholic Dogma.* Translated by Patrick Lynch. St. Louis, Missouri: B. Herder Book Company, 1954.

Parrinder, Geoffrey. *Jesus in the Qur'an.* London: One World Press, 2013.

Pascal, Blaise. *Pensees.* Translated by W. T. Trotter. New York: Random House, 1941.

Pelikan, Jaroslav. *Jesus Through the Centuries: His Place in the History of Culture.* New Haven: Yale University Press, 1985.

Perkins, Pheme. *Introduction to the Synoptic Gospels.* Grand Rapids, Michigan: Wm. B. Eerdmans Publishing Company, 2007.

Porton, Gary G. *GOYIM: Gentiles and Israelites in Mishnah-Tosefta.* Atlanta, Georgia: Scholars Press, 1988.

Powell, Mark. *Jesus as a Figure In History.* Louisville: Westminster John Knox Press, 1988.

Prothero, Stephen. *American Jesus: How the Son of God Became a National Icon.* New York: Farrar, Straus and Giroux, 2003.

———— *God is Not One: the Eight Rival Religions that run the World—and Why Their Differences Matter.* New York: Harper Collins, 2010.

Rhoads, David M. *Israel in Revolution 6–74 C.E.: A Political History Based on the Writings of Josephus*. Philadelphia: Fortress Press, 1976.

Rhoads, David, Joanna Dewey, and Donald Michie. *Mark as Story: An Introduction to the Narrative of the Gospel*. Minneapolis, MN: Augsburg Fortress Press, 2012.

Robinson, George. *Essential Judaism: A Complete Guide to Beliefs, Customs, and Rituals*. New York: Pocket Books, 2000.

Sanders, E. P. *The Historical Figure of Jesus*. London: Penguin Books, 1993.

Sandmel, Samuel. *We Jews and Jesus*. Woodstock, VT: First SkyLight Paths, 2006.

Schäfer, Peter. *Jesus in the Talmud*. Princeton: Princeton University Press, 2007.

Schweitzer, Albert. *The Quest for the Historical Jesus: A Critical Study of the Progress from Reimarus to Wrede*. New York: Macmillan, 1968.

Segal, Alan F., *Life After Death: A History of the Afterlife in the Religions of the West*. New York: Doubleday, 2004.

Shahak, Israel. *Jewish History Jewish Religion: The Weight of Three Thousand Years*. London: Pluto Press, 1994.

Shahak, Israel, and Norton Mezvinsky. *Jewish Fundamentalism in Israel*. London: Pluto Press, New edition, 2004.

Sharma, Arvind, editor. *Our Religions*. New York: Harper Collins, 1993.

Smith, Wilfred Cantwell. *Faith and Belief*. Princeton: Princeton University Press, 1979.

Stark, Rodney. *Discovering God: The Origins of the Great Religions and the Evolution of Belief*. New York: HarperOne, 2007.

Strong, John S. *Buddhisms: An Introduction*. London: One World Publications, 2015.

Tabor, James. *Paul and Jesus*. New York: Simon and Schuster, 2012.

Theissen, Gerd, and Annette Merz. *The Historical Jesus: A Comprehensive Guide*. Minneapolis: Fortress Press, 1998.

Tillich, Paul. *The Dynamics of Faith*. New York: Harper and Row, 1957.

Vermes, Geza. *Jesus and the World of Judaism*. London: SCM Press ltd, 1983.

Watt, W. Montgomery. *Islam and Christianity Today*. London: Routledge and Kegan Paul, 1993.

White, L. Michael. *From Jesus to Christianity*. New York: Harper Collins, 2004.

Wright, Robert. *The Evolution of God*. New York: Little, Brown and Company, 2009.

Index

Abelard, Pierre, 27–28
Abou El Fadl, Khaled, 96
Adam and Eve, 6, 23, 85, 106
Ahmad, 60, 64
Ahmad, Mirza, 64
Ahmadiyya, 62, 64
Allah (God), 67n2
anatta, 83, 84
annica, 83
Antiquities (Josephus), 16, 40
Anselm, 27
Aquinas, Thomas, 30
Arab, 55–56
Arabic, 67n2
Aristotle, 19
Arius, 20, 21, 22, 23
artha, 74
atonement theories, 26–12; satisfaction, 27; moral influence, 27, 27–28
Augustine, 24–26
avatar, 74, 77
axial age, 89n2

Babylonian Exile, 38
Babylonian Talmud, 39, 41
Balaam in Hell, 43, 104
Ballou, Hosea, 111
Barth, Karl, 111
Battle of Tours, 56
Bauer, Bruno, 47
Bhagavad Gita, 74, 78

bhakti yoga, 73, 74
Bible, 28, 29, 30
Biddle, John, 30
Bill of Rights, 32
Blasphemy Act, 30
Brahman, 73
Brahmo Samaj, 77
Buddha, the, 81
Buddhism, 81; as supreme wisdom, 88; *dukkha* (suffering), 83, 90n6; fate of others, 94–95; four noble truths, 83; four passing sights, 7, 82; impermanence of all, 82, 84; *nirvana*, 83, 84; noble eightfold path, 83, 84; no soul doctrine (*anatta*), 84; *tanha* (thirst, craving), 83

Calvin, John, 28, 30, 109
Carey, William, 75
Carthage, Council of, 26
caste system, 77, 83
Chalcedon, Council of, 24
Charles II, 31
Christ of faith, 8, 52
Christianity, 8, 18, 34n3; anthropology, 70; cosmology, 69–70; definition of, 11, 52; fate of others, 104–112; story, 42; supremacist, 106
Christology, 21
colonialism, 75
Confessions (Augustine), 25

Constantine, 24, 41
Constitution, United States, 31
Cook, Michael, 44
Cosmology, 69; Christian, 69–70; Hindu, 71
Cybele, 15
Cyrus, 38

Dalai Lama, 88
David, King, 40
Dawkins, Richard, 112
Dead Sea Scrolls, 39
death, problem of, ix, 13
Demeter, 15
Dhamapala, Anagarika, 87
dharma, 72, 75
diaspora, 39
Divine Law, 51–52
Docetism, 20, 21, 22, 23
dualism, 22
dukkha (suffering), 90n6

Ebionites, 17
Edict of Milan, 41
Edict of Thessalonica, 41
end times, end of days, 63
English Act of Toleration, 31
Enlightenment, 28, 32
Epicurean, 7
Epistle to Yemen (Maimonides), 45
Errors of the Trinity (Servetus), 29
Essenes, 39
evil, problem of, 21, 86
ex nihilo, 70
exclusivist religion, 93

faith, 25
Fall, the, 25, 27, 106
fate of others: Buddhism, 94–95; Catholicism, 107–109; Hinduism, 94; Islam, 95–100; Judaism, 100–104; Protestantism, 109–110
Fiddler on the Roof, 6
four noble truths, 83
four passing sights, 7, 82
Fox, George, 31
Fucan, Fabian, 85

Gandhi, Mohandas, 76, 78–79

Gehenna (Hell), 104, 109
Geiger, Abraham, 47–48
Ghazali, Abu Hamid, 98
Gnostic, Gnosticism, 20, 21, 22
Godse, Nathuram, 79
Gospels, 17–18, 40, 46
grace, 25; in Catholicism, 25, 109; in Protestantism, 25, 109
Grand Unifying Theory, 19, 78
Great Man question, 1–2
Greek religion, 14–15
Guide of the Perplexed (Maimonides), 44
Gyatso, Tenzin (Dalai Lama), 88

Hades, 15
Hadith, 63
Hanh, Thich Nhat, 89
Hazm, Ibn, 97
Heaven and Hell, 104, 109
Hellenism, 12, 19, 39
henotheism, 19
Hick, John, 111
Hinduism: bhakti yoga, 73, 74; Brahman, 73; caste system, 72, 76; *dharma*, 72, 75; fate of others, 94; Hindu Anthropology, 71–72; Hindu Cosmology, 71; jnana yoga, 73; *karma*, 72; karma marga, 73; *moksha* (release), 72, 75; reform Hinduism, 76; *samsara* (rebirth), 72
Historical Jesus, 8
Holocaust, 102
human beings: Christian view, 70; Hindu view, 71–72

inclusivist religion, 93
Isis, 15
Islam, 55, 66, 67n2; Hadith, 63; heaven and hell, 96; fate of others, 95–100; Quran, 24, 55, 57

"J" word, the, 49
James, brother of Jesus, 16
James, William, 65
Jefferson, Thomas, 12, 32–33, 77
Jefferson's Bible, 33
Jerusalem Temple, 38
Jesus in Christianity, 11; as Savior, 8

Jesus in Judaism: as bastard, 42, 43; as miracle worker, 44; in Hell, 43; Jewish man of his day, 49, 52; no virgin birth, 50; not divine, 50; not Messiah, 50; not resurrected, 43, 44, 50; son of Jewish Mary, 42; son of Roman soldier, 42, 43; stoned by fellow Jews, 43, 45; teacher of morality, 49

Jesus in Islam, 57; born of virgin Mary, 58; death of, 61–62; names for Jesus, 57; not divine, 57, 66; not crucified, 58, 61; not resurrected, 58; not savior, 67; messenger of God, 59, 61, 67; miracle worker, 60

Jesus in Hinduism: avatar (incarnation), 77; not sole incarnation, 77, 78; teacher of morality, 77, 78, 79

Jesus in Buddhism, 81; a simple man, 87, 88; not resurrected, 86, 87; teacher of morality, 88; unlearned, 87, 88

jihad, 64

jnana yoga, 73

Johnson, Paul, 6

Josephus, Flavius, 16, 40

Jost, Isaac, 46

Judaism, 13, 38–39; Conservative, 100; fate of human beings, 100–102; fate of gentiles, 102–104; fate of others, 100–104; Orthodox, 51, 100; Reconstructionist, 100, 103; Reform, 48, 100, 102, 103

judgment, 101

Ka'ba, 55

Kabbalah, 101

kama, 74

Kamasutra, 74

karma, 72, 83, 84

karma marga, 73

Khadija, 56

Kierkegaard, Soren, 79n6

King David, 40

Klausner, Joseph, 48, 49

Law, 20

Life and Morals of Jesus of Nazareth (Jefferson), 33

Life of Jesus, The (Strauss), 47

Light of Asia (Arnold), 82

Limbo, 105, 109

Luther, Martin, 28, 30, 44, 109

Mahdi, 64

Maimonides, Moses, 44–45, 101; on Jesus, 45

Manichaeism, 25

Marcion, 20, 21, 22–23

Mary (Miriam): in Christianity, 58; in Islam, 58; in Judaism, 42, 43

Mary Magdalene, 42

maya (illusion), 72

Mecca, 55, 56

Medina (Yathrib), 56

memes, 5, 6, 66

Messiah, 14, 17, 40, 59

messianic hope, 14

Mishnah, 113n20

moksha (release), 72, 75

monism, 19

monotheism, 19

Montefiore, Claude, 48–49

Moses, 55, 59

Muhammad, 55, 59, 60

Murray, John, 111

Muslim, 67n2; exclusivists, 97; inclusivists, 98; pluralists, 97; universalist, 99–100

mysticism, 65, 101

mythopoeic mind, 3

Myths, 3–4, 6, 47; broken myth, 4; etiological, 15; live and dead, 4; natural literalism, 4; reactive literalism, 4

Nero, 18

Neusner, Jacob, 49–50

New Testament, 23

Nicaea, Council of, 24

Nicene Creed, 24

nirvana, 83

Old Testament, 13, 23, 38

omen about Jesus, 87

On the Jews and Their Lies (Luther), 44

Oral Law, 39

Origen, 110

original sin, 25, 26, 51

Osiris, 15

Pandera, 42, 43–44
Pascal, Blaise, 91
Pascal's wager, 91–92
Paul the Apostle, ix, 16–17, 18–20, 42, 86
Pelagius, 26
Pelikan, Jaroslav, 28
Persephone, 15
Persians, 38
Peter the Apostle, 16
Pharisees, 13, 39, 101
Plato, 19, 34n19, 84, 102
pluralists, 93, 97
polytheism, 19, 55
Pope Boniface VIII, 107
Pope Innocent III, 107
Pope John XXIII, 109
Pope Pius IX, 107
predestination, 110
Priestley, Joseph, 32
Protestants: fate of others, 109–110; on grace, 25; Reformation, 28, 45; universalists, 111
Purgatory, 104, 105, 109

Quakers, 31
Quran (Qur'an, Koran), 24, 55, 57

Rahula, 81
Ramakrishna, 76, 77
Reimarus, Hermann, 46
Religion: as memeplexes, 5, 6; as stories, 3, 5, 6; as tribalism, x; exclusivist, 93; inclusivist, 93; market place model, ix; pluralist, 93; salvation, 7; supremacist, x, 92, 93; universalist, 93
resurrection of the body, 70, 100–101
Robinson, George, 103
Roman Catholic Church, 28; sacramental grace, 107; fate of others, 107–109
Roman religion, 14–15
Rorschach test, 96
Roy, Ram Mohan, 76, 76–77
Rumi, Jalaluddin, 65

sacraments: in Catholicism, 107; in Protestantism, 109
Sadducees, 13, 39
salvation, 7
samsara, 72, 83, 84

Sandmel, Samuel, 17, 46, 49
Saraswati, 76
Schäfer, Peter, 43, 53n9
science, 25, 29, 30, 44
scriptures, 2
Secher, Allen, 49
Second Vatican Council, 93, 108
Septuagint, 13
Sermon on the Mount, 78
Servetus, Michael, 30
shahada, 66
Shema, 113n19
sheol, 101
Shi-ite (Shia), 64
Simon Bar Kokhba, 38
Simon of Cyrene, 24, 62
sin, 25, 26
sola fide, 109
sola gratia, 109
sola scriptura, 109
Son of God, 14, 42
sons of god, 14
soul, 70, 84, 102
Southern Baptist Convention, 33, 114n39
Spinoza, Baruch, 29
Stephen, 16
Stoics, 19
Strauss, David Friedrich, 47
Sufis, 64, 65
Sunni, 64
suttee (sati), 77

Talmud, 41, 42, 53n7, 103–104; Babylonian, 39, 41; banned, 44
tanha (thirst, craving), 83
Tawrah (Torah), 59
Taymiyya, 99–100
Tevye, 6
The Fall, 25, 27, 106
Tillich, Paul, 4
Timaeus (Plato), 34n19
Titus, 43; in Hell, 103
Toledot Yeshu (History of Jesus), 43–44, 45, 60
Torah, 20, 38, 39, 40, 41, 42, 51
Tosefta, 113n20
Tours, battle of, 56
Trinity, 30, 42
Tyche (Fate, Fortuna), 13

Unam Sanctum (one holy), 107
Unitarians, 30
Universalists, 30

Vatican II, 93, 108
Vedas, 71
Virgin Birth, 30, 42; in Judaism, 42; in Islam, 58
Vivekananda, 76, 78

We Jews and Jesus (Sandmel), 50

World to come, 14, 101, 104

Yathrib (Medina), 56
Yen, Sheng, 88
yogas, 73–74, 75

Zealots, 39
Zeus, 15, 19
Zhixu, Ouyi, 86
Zionism, 48, 49
Zoroastrian, 38, 63, 100